A Year Off...
A Year On?

Eileen De'Ath
Tessa Doe
Helen Evans
Debbie Steel

Student Helpbook Series

Lifetime Careers

A Year Off... A Year On? - seventh edition
This edition revised January 2002
Published by Lifetime Careers Publishing, 7 Ascot Court, White Horse
Business Park, Trowbridge BA14 0XA

© Lifetime Careers Wiltshire Ltd, 2002

ISBN 1 902876 32 6

Printed and bound by Cromwell Press Ltd, Trowbridge
Cover design by Jane Norman

About the authors

This seventh edition of *A Year Off... A Year On?* has been produced by the team of authors responsible for the widely used CLIPS series of careers information leaflets. Eileen De'Ath, Tessa Doe, Helen Evans and Debbie Steel have also written, revised and edited other student handbooks and options guides as well as a range of materials for adults returning to education and for students with special needs. Between them, they have broad and varied experience of the worlds of education, employment and careers guidance. They have also all travelled widely, which has been very useful in compiling some of the advice in the latter chapters of this book!

Acknowledgements

Jacki Ciereszko for her help in collating the information, and for desktop publishing the end result.

Other Lifetime Careers Wiltshire staff, who helped to find individual profilees and other contacts.

The many contributors, named in the text, who have shared their experiences with us by writing the profiles.

The admissions officers and tutors from the following institutions who participated in our survey:

Sheffield Hallam University
University of Leicester
University of Warwick
University of the West of England
University of Wolverhampton
University of Bath
College of York St John
University of Huddersfield

Buckinghamshire Chilterns University College
University of Central England in Birmingham
University of Wales, Bangor
Heriot-Watt University
Nottingham Trent University
Aston University

The following employers of graduates who took part in our employers' survey:

B K R Haines Watts Accountants
BAE Systems
BP
Bureau Van Dijk Electronic Publishing Ltd
Centre for Applied Microbiology and Research
Compass Group
Croda International
Dorset County Council
European Commission
Future Publishing
Halifax plc
Harrods Ltd
Hitachi Europe Ltd
Jone Lang LaSalle

Kerry Group
Kimberley-Clark Ltd
Majestic Wine
Mars UK
Metropolitan Police Service
NHS Management Training Scheme
Oracle Corporation UK Ltd
Pilkington plc
Pitney Bowes Ltd
RM
Thames Water
Towers Perrin
Transco
W H Smith Group
Wilco International

Contents

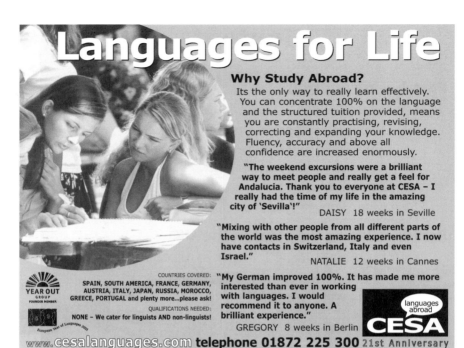

Introduction

About this book

It seems that an ever-increasing number of students now take a year out between school and further or higher education. Others take time out between school and work, or between graduation and employment. Adults may decide that they need a year or more doing something totally different in mid-career, perhaps just to refresh themselves before carrying on with their lives, or possibly leading to a complete change of direction. Even after retirement, more people are opting to spend a year or more travelling or doing voluntary work overseas.

In a world of short, fixed-term contracts and the expectation of several career changes in a lifetime, the prospect of a year out is both tempting and practicable, but the choice of what to do and when is as difficult as ever. *A Year Off... A Year On?* offers a balanced mix of background information and advice and listings of organisations which offer paid or voluntary work, travel or study opportunities in the UK and overseas. The book is largely geared toward the traditional pre-university gap year student, but is also intended to be of use to all other age groups.

There can be some problems and disadvantages relating to taking a gap year, but the advantages would appear to be much greater. Certainly our surveys of employers and admissions tutors show a largely positive attitude to a well-spent year out. Individual case studies in the book are testimony to the rich experiences, increased skills and confidence and broadened horizons that a successful gap year can bring.

Inclusion of any organisation or scheme in this book is not a recommendation.

We hope that you enjoy this book, and that it helps you to find your ideal year-out experience.

Eileen De'Ath, Tessa Doe, Helen Evans and Debbie Steel

N.B. Some costs are quoted in francs, marks etc. This information was collected before the introduction of the euro. We're afraid you'll have to do your own calculations!

Chapter 1
Time out options
- what, where, when?

There are many and varied options open to anyone seeking to take a year out. You will find full details of most of them in the later chapters of this book. Your choice will depend on several factors:

- **do you wish to spend a whole year on one option** - or to split the year between, say, work experience and travel, voluntary work and a language course or any other combination?

- **do you want to stay in the UK or to travel** - and if so how far afield?

- **what are your domestic and other commitments** - can and should you move away from home?

- **what is your financial situation** - do you need to earn money or can you afford to spend some?

- **what are your future career plans** - should you aim for relevant experience?

- **what do you have to offer** - are you suited to voluntary work, caring for the community or the environment, or are your abilities best utilised in the commercial or industrial sector?

- **what do you wish to gain from your experience** - an adventure, improved career prospects, independence, a break from your studies, confidence, new skills, or to see the world?

Whether you wish to stay in the UK, or to travel to Europe or beyond, the options can be divided into:

- paid employment
- voluntary work
- learning or studying - whether leading to recognised qualifications or not
- travelling - organised or independent.

Paid employment

Whether your main objective is to gain experience or to raise some cash to support your studies, the possibilities for paid employment are almost as varied for gap year jobseekers as for people seeking permanent work. Short-term seasonal work - at hotels and holiday centres in the summer or in shops in the run-up to Christmas, for example - can be a useful source of income to subsidise time spent travelling or doing voluntary work. Other opportunities are available at home or overseas to fill the whole year. If you are already in work but want to travel, your employer may be able to find you a temporary job abroad - to investigate new overseas markets, or to work for a foreign subsidiary for example. Some large employers have specially organised gap year employment schemes for able students, sometimes linked to sponsorship or vacation work during your course. The 'Year in Industry' scheme has the cooperation of a number of major employers in this country.

UK citizens are free to travel and work in the European Union, but visas and permits must be obtained to work in most other countries. There are organisations which will both help you to find work and to get the right documents. See chapters 6 and 9 for ideas and information.

For some courses and careers, for example social work, nursing, paramedical careers and conservation work, relevant experience is an advantage, or even a requirement. Our employers' survey in chapter 4 concludes that employers in most areas of work are particularly impressed by relevant work experience.

Voluntary work

Voluntary organisations expect you to be fully committed and enthusiastic about the work undertaken. Voluntary work may be in the community among children, the elderly, people with disabilities, the disadvantaged, the sick or the homeless, or it can mean working on environmental or conservation projects, often out of doors. All types of voluntary work are available both in the UK and abroad, for periods ranging from a week to two years. You may receive free or subsidised board and lodging, travel expenses and pocket money. Some schemes in the developing countries require you to find £2500 or more to cover your expenses before you are accepted. Other schemes may pay the equivalent of a basic wage in the host country, although the ethos is still that of voluntary work. See chapters 7 and 10.

Study

To spend a gap year studying might sound a bit like a busman's holiday, but studying a different subject in an environment that is new to you can be both enjoyable and useful. Time spent learning secretarial or computing skills, for example, can be of great benefit in your future career. You could study for Teaching English as a Foreign Language (TEFL) qualifications, or perhaps gain a diploma in some alternative therapy, or sports coaching. All of these qualifications can be used to find paid employment at any stage in your career. You can spend time abroad, perhaps living with a family, studying a country's language and culture informally, or you could attend more formal language and summer schools or spend a full academic year at a school or university overseas. If you are about to embark on a vocational degree course, you might enjoy using your gap year to study art history, astronomy, literature or music - or even beekeeping - something that you feel will enrich your quality of life. Why not? See chapters 8 and 11 for ideas.

There are a number of European Union exchange programmes which enable students to spend some time studying in another European country, while taking a UK degree or HND. There are also exchange schemes for students still at school.

Travel

If you want to see more of the UK, Europe or the rest of the world, you can choose between travelling with an organised group or independently, alone or with friends. The pros and cons of different ways of travelling are discussed in chapter 13. You will need to do plenty of planning and preparation to get the most out of your travels, and you may need to find paid work or sponsorship first to support you. Many of the organisations which offer voluntary or paid work abroad allow time off to travel independently while on their scheme, which could be another way of seeing the world.

Chapter 12 and 13 give information about travel agents and tour operators that specialise in adventure holidays, small-group expeditions, student travel, long-haul flights and around-the-world itineraries. You will find addresses of embassies in Part 5.

When to take time out?

The most popular time to take a year out is as a gap year between school and university or college. Many other students take their gap year at the end of their studies, before starting in employment, and a few between year 11 and employment or further education. Employers and admissions tutors are generally positive about gap years for students. But time out is possible at any time in your career - between jobs, or as unpaid leave or a sabbatical sponsored by your employer. It may be hard to envisage dropping everything and going abroad for a year when you have a house, a job and the cat and dog to worry about, but nothing is impossible. Banks, building societies and the Inland Revenue can all offer advice about the financial implications of a career break. A year or two between retiring and really settling down to the pipe and slippers routine is also a possibility; Voluntary Service Overseas, for instance, accepts volunteers up to the age of 68.

Deferred UCAS entry

If you intend to take time out before going on to higher education, you will need to consider when you will apply to university via UCAS (Universities and Colleges Admissions Service). It is possible to apply to university for deferred entry. Students apply to UCAS between September and January with the intention of starting their course the following September/October. Rather than starting your course the following year, you can opt to defer it to the next year and take a year out in between.

Alternatively, you can apply to higher education institutions after you receive your A level/BTEC National/AVCE (vocational A level)/Highers results. This means, though, that you will have to keep an eye on your applications during your year out. If applicable for your chosen course, you may have to be available to attend interviews from January to March of your year out. It is more sensible to apply for deferred entry. You can then relax during your year out knowing that you have a place in higher education confirmed. You will not have to spend any of your time out researching courses, filling in the UCAS form and attending interviews.

If you apply for deferred entry, you will need to explain what you intend to do in your year out on your UCAS form. Admissions tutors want to know that you have thought through what you want to do and achieve, and that you will be using your time constructively. It is, therefore, important that you plan your year out well ahead. See chapter 5 for admissions tutors' views and advice on what to put on your application form.

Chapter 2
Advantages and disadvantages of taking time out

Whether you plan to take a year out between school and further or higher education or employment, after graduation, or during your career, there are some negative and positive aspects that you need to consider. How much you benefit from the experience will be largely down to you - both in actually making the most of your gap year, and in being able to communicate what you have gained and its relevance to prospective employers, colleges or universities.

If you spend the time constructively, you are almost certain to gain in terms of experience, confidence and communication skills. But be aware that a few employers may be traditional in their attitudes and view a year out as proof that you are indecisive, uncommitted to a career or even just plain idle. You'll need to convince such employers that your experiences will be of benefit to their organisation, as well as to you personally.

You might find it difficult to get back into a routine, or you may not enjoy the insecurity of temporary work, or the basic living standards of a voluntary placement, or working with people you may feel you have nothing in common with. You may simply get homesick for friends and family.

Do think very carefully about the choices you make, taking your own strengths, weaknesses and preferences into account.

The advantages

If you still have doubts about the direction of your future education and career, a gap year can give you the chance of work experience - paid or voluntary - or a period of study which may clarify your ideas.

Relevant paid employment in a gap year is highly rated by employers of graduates, and work experience is a requirement for some higher education or professional courses. In any case, such experience will make your job application stand out compared to those from people who have experienced little outside school and university.

With life on a student loan to face in the future, a few months' salary in the bank will be most welcome.

Voluntary or paid work experience of any kind will improve your ability to work with others, your communication and organisational skills, your ability to work on your own initiative and your sense of responsibility.

Travel really does broaden the mind. Experience of different cultures, befriending people of other nationalities and backgrounds, improving your language skills, and coping with anything from minor inconveniences to major hazards will do wonders for your self-confidence and flexibility.

A year away from academic life may increase your enthusiasm for a further three or more years of study, and make you less likely to 'drop-out'.

An adventurous and worthwhile gap year can give you memories and experiences that you will look back on as one of the most exciting and rewarding times of your life. It is an opportunity to 'make a difference'.

The disadvantages

It may take time to get back into the routine of work or study; the more exciting your year out, the harder this might be.

Some subjects, like maths, technology and science, are more difficult than others to pick up again where you left off. This is one area where people who go straight from school into employment or higher education may have an advantage over you in the short term - but you should be able to catch up.

Timing can be a problem. If you are looking for work, try to be available before the mass of school- and college-leavers come onto the job market. Unless you are returning to work from a sabbatical, or you have deferred entry to a job, you will have to allow time to apply for jobs and attend interviews.

You won't be able to claim Jobseeker's Allowance if you are a full-time student, and the rules for part-time study are quite complicated. Voluntary workers can only claim JSA if they are genuinely seeking full-time work and willing to give up their voluntary placement if a paid job materialises.

If you do not have deferred entry to a higher education course, you will need to start the UCAS application procedure during your year out, and to be available for interviews if necessary. This will restrict how much travelling you can include in your gap year.

You may end your gap year in debt, rather than in profit.

Be prepared to be a year behind your contemporaries in terms of salary and promotion prospects.

If you are still in doubt, speak to local agencies such as the careers/ Connexions service, benefit offices and volunteer bureaux. Teachers and college tutors may well be able to help you, as they will have anecdotal evidence from other students. Try to find people who have had experience of a gap year to discuss your doubts with. Most of all, be honest with yourself about your motivation and capabilities.

In this book, we've included case-studies of people who have taken a variety of time out options. Their stories will help you to envisage what a gap year can be like, and you can read in their own words what they have gained, what the difficulties were and how they overcame them. If you don't take a year out when the opportunity presents itself, you may spend the rest of your life wondering 'what if....'

Chapter 3
Planning ahead and finance

If you intend to take some time out, you should aim to start researching the possibilities open to you at least a year beforehand. For some options, you will need to raise finance, and you will need to apply early to most of the organisations offering opportunities. If you intend to apply to higher education, you will have to have some idea of what you plan to do a year before, so you can defer your entry and explain your intentions to admissions tutors.

You should consider your time out as a whole; if you need to raise a considerable amount of money, you may have to spend the first three or four months of your year out working full-time. You may want to build time for travel into your year, so you need to consider how you will fund this. Whatever you are planning to do, some money will be required for accommodation, food, insurance, kit and, of course, to have some fun!

Don't let your concern about finance put you off. Surveys have shown that many people who consider a gap year fail to follow it through because of money worries. A year off often costs less than you may think. With effort, taking time out is a real possibility for people from all backgrounds. Later in this chapter, you will read about the range of ways money can be raised.

If you decide to find paid work in the UK

It is unlikely that you will need to save money beforehand, but you will need to start applying to organisations and contacting employers about six months before you hope to start work. You will need to compile a CV, and find out what the employment situation is like in the area in which you intend to work. You may want to apply for jobs at holiday centres, as an au pair or teaching English as a foreign language, and for jobs in these areas early application is essential. You may also need to gain some relevant experience before applying. If you plan to work in shops, hotels, restaurants or on building sites, you could try getting a part-time job and increase your hours into a full-time job later. If you intend to do temporary office work, you might need to develop some basic office skills before you sign on with agencies, in order to increase your chances of employment.

If you plan to find paid work abroad

You should research organisations that offer opportunities and apply early. If you plan to fix up your position independently, find out about the employment, or unemployment, situation and which organisations you should contact when looking for work. In most non-English-speaking countries, you will need a reasonable understanding of the local language for most jobs; for some jobs, you must have very good written and spoken language skills. Often, you will need to pay for your own air fare and insurance. Exceptions to this include au pair work, or working as a summer camp counsellor in the USA with organisations like Bunacamp or Camp America, where air fare and insurance are usually paid for you; these opportunities are popular so apply early.

If you intend to find voluntary work in the UK or abroad

If you decide to do voluntary work, whether it is some form of social work in the community, joining workcamps or conservation work, you will usually have to pay the costs of travelling there, and insurance. Once you are working, pocket money is often provided, and board and lodging may be free.

Those aiming at voluntary work overseas may have to pay an organisation a fee towards the expenses of providing your placement; this can amount to a substantial sum - £2500 or more. You will also need sufficient personal spending money - perhaps including enough to fund some travelling after your placement. Don't forget you may need to buy essential clothes and equipment, such as a decent backpack, sleeping bag, etc beforehand.

Conduct some research on any organisation you are considering – they don't all have a good reputation. Find out what support will be available from them when you are on your placement, how much they charge and what is included in that price (e.g. healthcare, training, emergency back-up, help with fund-raising...). It is a good idea to ask for the contact details of past volunteers so that you can speak to them about their experiences. Ask about the percentage of people who drop out before the end of their programme. Remember that you should choose the organisation which best meets your needs – you can even opt to organise your own placement.

Intending volunteers find creative ways to help raise funds. These include temporary or part-time work, of course; undertaking sponsored activities; or raising money through sales of goods from cakes to second-hand clothes. In particular, it may be fruitful to research any local charities or trust funds that can be of help. Each year, £1000s of available sponsorship money goes unclaimed! Your local reference library may be able to provide information. Your school or college could have ideas about organisations to approach, gained from the experience of previous gap year students. Sometimes local organisations, which raise money for good causes, may support you, perhaps on the understanding that you give a talk about your experience afterwards. Most importantly, as mentioned above, organisations offering voluntary placements often offer advice about fundraising.

There are many and varied ways of raising the necessary funds. Read one volunteer's account in this chapter.

If you intend to study

There is some scope for scholarships but you need to research these thoroughly and apply early. Useful books to refer to are listed in Part 5, and should be available in university and college careers libraries and in large local libraries. If you are considering studying in Europe, there are European Union-funded programmes, in particular the Socrates-Erasmus and Leonardo programmes. These enable higher education students to spend time on study or work placements in other parts of Europe, and are mentioned in more detail in Part 3.

If you want to travel/join expeditions

You will need to save a fairly substantial amount of money; you may need to work in the UK for several months first. Expeditions or adventure holidays can cost in the region of £2500 or more; if this option is your choice you'll need plenty of time to raise the cash. You could consider some of the ideas mentioned previously in this chapter.

In conclusion...

Most of the options you can choose require money, so it's worth getting a part-time job during your school/college studies or, if you are established in a career, saving as much of your salary as you can. Most people who take time out do not have access to large sums from sponsorship or scholarships, and rely entirely on their own finances. They use their own initiative to raise funds, live sparingly and save as much as possible from temporary work. Even Prince William found various ways of raising money to fund his recent gap year, including organising a water polo match! So, get saving, get planning, get applying and the world's your oyster.

Profile   **Anthony Putt**
Raising the Finances!

'It can be a daunting prospect, realising that you have to fund your whole gap year. Whether teaching in Thailand, canoeing in Canada or skiing in Switzerland make sure you begin saving early and planning how you will pay for the year.

I found there were endless sources of funding. With a little effort and commitment many people were more than willing to help. Initially I wrote to local companies from supermarkets to car dealers. Most were willing to pledge the odd five or ten pounds towards my year out, teaching in West Africa. I was awarded the school travel prize, and encouraged to write to local churches which proved an invaluable source. My 'Africa Account' was off the ground.

As my pool of local contacts dried up I realised a little effort on my part might be needed. With help from family and friends I raised over £400 in a tennis tournament, which many others and I enjoyed. In February, before I left for foreign shores, I took a part in the local pantomime, 'Beauty and the Beast', and the group gave me £250 for travelling and teaching from the pantomime proceeds.

Of course there are always the old fashioned ways of funding your year out: hard work and begging. I spent a month working in a meat factory, saving £100 each week. Fortunately my grandparents were also kind enough to make a contribution to my fund.

Friends I shared my gap year with found other sources. Car boot sales proved a great way of raising cash and getting rid of old junk. Dance events, summer balls and school discos took lots of organisation, but earned a good lump sum in one evening. Of course you don't have to take all the pressure of organising an event on your own. Getting together with other 'gappers' and splitting the proceeds or recruiting volunteers is a good idea.

I varied my fund raising approaches, and learned not to rely on one or two sources. As I reached my target I realised how much hard work and effort it had taken. I had learned how to plan ahead, and when the final figure was reached I was satisfied and secure in the knowledge that a great year lay ahead.'

Chapter 4
Employers' views

When planning your year out, think ahead to the time when you will be jobhunting after completion of your studies. How do you think the activities you undertake will impress a potential employer? Can you adapt your plans to make them more relevant to your career, without diminishing your own enjoyment and satisfaction? What will employers expect you to have gained from a year out? The chances are that if you find the experience challenging and rewarding, then your future employer will gain from it too. But a wasted year is not going to impress anyone.

Those who intend to take a year out after further or higher education will be wise to apply for jobs while still on the course. You may find the ideal job with an employer who is willing to keep it open for you for a year. Large firms with a regular intake of graduate trainees may well be able to do this, particularly if your year out activities are seen to be constructive and relevant to their needs. And if you don't find such an opening, at least you will have had some useful application and interview experience for a year's time!

Those already in work, who intend to return to a similar position after a year out, should approach their present employer about taking a sabbatical or unpaid leave. If this is not possible or desirable, then try to keep in touch with developments in your field of work while you are away. Working practices change so rapidly today, that being a year behind the times could be seen as a great disadvantage. This can be counterbalanced, though, by the likely enhancement of your leadership and communication skills, adaptability, initiative etc, which can come from a constructive year out.

25

Survey of employers' attitudes

We received 31 responses to our survey of employers, from organisations of varying size which recruit graduates, spread fairly evenly among the financial and business sector, manufacturing, engineering/technology, public sector and service industries. (See acknowledgements at the front of the book.) We asked about their attitudes to applicants who have taken time out, either before or after higher education. Most of the comments made will also apply to employers who recruit for non-graduate positions.

Question: Would you treat applicants who had taken a year out more favourably than, less favourably than or no differently from other applicants?

A majority of about two thirds of respondents said such applicants would be treated no differently, with about a third opting for more favourably, although these answers were sometimes qualified by a statement that the applicant would need to have done something worthwhile. Only one respondent said they would look less favourably - but only on applicants who had taken a year out after higher education.

Question: Which type of year-out experience would you most value?

24 of the respondents said paid employment relevant to their organisation would be most valued. Gaining new skills or qualifications was the second most popular option, with other paid employment third and voluntary work and travel bringing up the rear. One employer distinguished between independent and challenging travel (highly rated) and non-challenging travel (lowly rated). However, it was apparent from some comments that all options would be valued if the applicant could prove that the year out had given them skills, experiences or attitudes which would benefit the employer.

Question: What do you see as the advantages of a year out?

Most frequently mentioned were greater maturity and increased skills (such as communication, teamwork, negotiation, leadership etc as well as practical skills). Broadening of horizons and perspective was seen as the next greatest advantage (interestingly, as travel alone was the least favoured gap-year experience yet seems to offer great opportunities in this field). Other gains mentioned were greater adaptability and flexibility, improved languages skills, common sense, being more focused, greater planning and organisational skills and having increased confidence/independence/self-reliance. One employer quoted 'more realistic expectations of the world of work' as being an advantage. Another said gap-year applicants were likely to feel more settled and not likely to assume 'the grass is greener' elsewhere.

Question: What do you see as the disadvantages of a year out?

Eight of the respondents gave an unqualified 'none' in answer to this question. Others suggested possible disadvantages were getting the 'travel bug' and not being able to settle (the opposite of one of the answers to the previous question!), loss of skills or business knowledge, getting out of the work/study habit, loss of career focus and difficulty in catching up. The point was also made several times that a poorly thought-out or wasted gap year would be difficult to justify to an employer. It could be seen as just 'a long holiday'. One employer pointed out that the selection process may take longer if the applicant spends a period of time overseas.

Question: Does your attitude vary according to the subject studied or the vacancy applied for?

Only two respondents said 'yes' to this. One stated that it would depend on the selection criteria for the particular job. The other spoke of the loss of functional skills for functional training (presumably of a technical or scientific nature) as opposed to the gaining of 'soft' skills useful for general management training.

Conclusions from the survey

The survey results show that, overall, employers appreciate the experience, maturity and competencies gained during a year out. It is up to you to make the most of packaging and selling the results of your own experiences to the employer in your CV and at interview. Don't be afraid to emphasise different aspects of what you have gained to suit the needs of different employers. Each vacancy requires a unique approach. Remember, interviewers particularly want evidence that your year out has given you:

- relevant work experience
- maturity and self-confidence
- communication, leadership and teamwork skills
- language skills
- initiative and self-reliance
- planning and organisational skills
- a broader perspective on life
- adaptability and flexibility.

In these times of student debt, earning money to help you through your course is likely to be a major advantage of a year out in your eyes. However, it may not seem so important to some employers, so emphasise the relevance of the work rather than its profitability! Don't just list the jobs; list the skills you gained from them.

If you have taken a year out after further or higher education, you may have a bit more difficulty in convincing the employer that you have not lost any of the skills and knowledge gained during your course, and are now ready to settle into your career. So, ensure that you make the most of all the advantages listed above to add weight to your application.

N.B. The European Commission was one employer surveyed. They did not answer the above questions because, as they pointed out, recruitment to the EC is by exam. However, they acknowledge that a gap year can be an excellent way to improve language skills and learn more about Europe or about a particular subject area, which can enhance an applicant's chances of success in the recruitment competition.

Chapter 5
Admissions tutors' views

Previous surveys of higher education admissions tutors have shown that, in general, they are positive about the idea of students taking a year out between school and higher education. We wanted to find out whether this is still the case. So, in the summer of 2001, we undertook a survey involving 53 admissions tutors and admissions officers from 14 higher education establishments (listed in the acknowledgements at the beginning of this book).

As well as providing an overall picture of admissions tutors' attitudes to students who take a year out, the survey also asked which gap year experiences are most valued by admissions staff, and which do not impress! We also asked if there were any particular problems or difficulties that gap year students may face when returning to education, and for any advice that tutors could offer.

The admissions tutors participating came from a wide range of subject areas, both academic and vocational. This included biological sciences, business, chemistry, computing, construction, design, economics, education, English, environmental sciences, media, languages, law, mathematics, performing arts, nursing and other health professions, physics, psychology and social sciences.

Do bear in mind that the views expressed are those of a relatively small sample of admissions tutors and officers. Nevertheless, we found that their views were, in the main, quite similar, with recurring themes of both encouragement and warning! Their answers to our questions provide some important messages to prospective gap-year students.

Question: What are your views regarding students who have taken, or are planning to take, a year out?

A large majority of respondents viewed taking a year out as an idea they positively welcomed. A few were more neutral, and some tutors expressed reservations, mostly about the usefulness or relevance of activities undertaken. A number said that it depends on the individual student. The words 'focused', 'mature' and 'confident' cropped up quite often, describing those who had completed a gap year. One or two tutors felt it necessary to point out that their positive attitude toward gap years did not mean that students who went straight from school to university would be viewed unfavourably. Some tutors commented that a year out could help students to decide on which course was right for them – presumably suggesting that applications should be made at the end of a gap year rather than before it.

Question: What types of gap-year experience do you most value?

Many tutors mentioned either course- or career-related experiences; relevant work experience being highly favoured in particular by admissions tutors for vocational courses, such as business, computing, technology and health. Improving foreign language skills was mentioned, not surprisingly, by modern languages tutors but also by others, such as those in business and management areas. However, one tutor thought that a gap-year experience was probably all the better for not being course-related! Several thought a combination of work (paid or voluntary) and travel was of high value. Many used words like well-planned, structured, constructive or purposeful to describe the ideal gap year. A lot of emphasis was placed on the interpersonal or transferable skills which could be developed during a year out, such as teamworking, communication, time management, leadership etc. One tutor reflected the views of a number of others by stating 'The experience itself is irrelevant in some ways, it's what the individual learns from it that is important'.

Question: What types of gap-year experience do you least value?

The recurring theme here was that tutors do not like unplanned, unproductive, unstructured, wasted gap years. Some used phrases like 'taking a long holiday', 'dossing around at home', 'hanging around Thai beaches' or 'bumming around Australia' as experiences they would not value. Pure hedonism does not go down well. Others expressed reservations about spending the year in unskilled work such as supermarket shelf-filling or working in fast-food outlets (poor old McDonalds gets several mentions). However, some respondents acknowledged that students may need to earn money by any (legal!) means available to support their studies. One tutor specified retaking

A levels when not absolutely necessary as a waste of a year. A few said that any type of gap-year experience could be of value.

Question: What do you expect students to tell you about their gap-year experiences/plans on their UCAS application form?

Most tutors look for a brief explanation of the applicant's aims and intentions for the year. They want to know what you will be doing, and how you hope to benefit and learn from it. Several tutors like applicants to explain the relevance of the year out to the course for which they are applying, and to their post-university career. Evidence of forethought and planning are appreciated.

If you are making your application after taking time out, tutors want to know what you have done and what skills, personal attributes and/or knowledge you have gained as a result. A few tutors mentioned that they need details of how you can be contacted.

One tutor thought this part of the application offered a good starting point for conversation at interview. Another (the only one!) would like to hear about the fun times as well as the learning experiences.

Question: What differences in attitude, if any, do you notice in students who have taken a gap year compared to those who start straight from school?

A small but vocal majority claimed that they do see a positive difference. Increased maturity and confidence, students being better focused, more committed and motivated and more able to settle down to a university career were the most frequent comments. Almost as many could not or would not generalise about differences. Only three quoted more negative attitudes in gap-year students, i.e. feeling threatened by timetables and required attendance, initial anxiety about returning to study, and a tendency to just drift away! These responses should be considered together with the answers to the next question.

Question: Are there any disadvantages to taking a year out, such as problems coping with a return to study?

A majority of tutors thought there were either no discernible disadvantages or did not wish to generalise. A few pointed out that difficulties in adapting to degree-level study can occur in any group of students, not just those who have taken a gap year. One or two felt that one year out made no difference to a student's ability to study, but a longer break did.

Possible disadvantages mentioned were: being broke again after earning money; finding it difficult to settle; loss of motivation (although in the previous question increased motivation was cited); the need to regain self-discipline for academic study.

One response pointed out that a good induction programme and personal tutorial system should iron out most problems for gap-year students as well as for others.

Question: Would you normally advise students to take a year out?

15 respondents gave an unqualified 'yes', and only two a firm 'no'. The rest said, in various ways, that it was up to the individual student and they would not offer advice. A number of these did feel that a gap year was usually of benefit, but added that it was not right for everyone.

Question: Any other advice or comments?

Being very busy people, most tutors did not offer any gems of wisdom, but there were some interesting answers, such as:

> *'Now that the gap year is so fashionable, don't feel pushed into it! Post-university gaps are also possible.'*

> *'Think about your objectives.'*

> *'Take a gap year, but use it wisely. Save some money!'*

> *'Don't drift.'*

> *'It is worth discussing with the admissions tutor of the course you are interested in and/or the university in general prior to making the decision of what to do during the year out.'*

> *'Make sure they have a good time – they'll probably never get another chance.'*

Responses relevant to specific subject areas

Management, computing, business etc

Admissions tutors for these subjects were particularly keen on students gaining relevant work experience, although they value other experiences too as long as the student gains useful skills as a result. One computing tutor thought a gap year was not a good idea 'because you need to get into the IT profession as early as possible'.

English and Languages

Experience overseas which enhances the student's ability in the language or languages they wish to study was, obviously, welcomed. Other experiences 'which help students to stand on their own two feet' were also valued, especially if the student could keep their language skills 'ticking over'. The University of Warwick says that English selectors prefer students to apply during rather than before their gap year.

Subjects related to maths, physical science and technology

There were several references to mathematical skills getting rusty. It was suggested that you should find a way of keeping up your skills and knowledge during your gap year; continue to read about the subject, revise what you did at A level, or find work that uses mathematical and/or scientific skills. One tutor particularly recommended laboratory work, while another valued any experience which combines technical content with people skills.

This group tended to be less enthusiastic about the benefits of a gap year, while still being generally in favour of the idea. Several felt it made no difference, or had no strong views either way.

Art, music, media, performing arts

Art and design students are encouraged by one tutor to use a gap year for 'visual research'. Perhaps surprisingly, music and performing arts are areas in which several tutors were not keen on students taking a gap year. Music tutors, particularly, are concerned that practical skills may suffer. The Birmingham Conservatoire (part of UCE) sent the following statement:

'We normally do not allow students to take a gap year. As our courses are all mainly performance-based, and as competition for the limited number of places available each year is so keen, we need to know that practical standards are likely to be at least maintained, and preferably developed during the period between entrance auditions and the start of the course. Therefore, candidates who are intending to take a year out normally have to re-audition the following year. (I say 'normally' because, occasionally, the gap-year activity may itself be likely to enhance a candidate's First Study abilities.)'

The University of Warwick's School of Theatre Studies 'can only consider gap year applications in exceptional cases' while the university on the whole welcomes gap-year applicants. Another respondent from a theatre, film and TV course thought that 'In a highly practical area such as ours, all would benefit'.

Social work, teaching, youth and community work etc

As many courses in social and youth and community work require entrants to be age 19 or over, with relevant work experience, a gap year is usually welcome. The year should preferably be spent in areas related to the course, such as working with children or communities, in health or social care, whether paid or voluntary.

Two tutors on teaching courses were keen that students should experience 'the wider world' outside education institutions – although there was also some concern that potential students might change their mind about teacher training!

The UCAS application should identify gap-year experiences that relate to the degree course.

Biology, health care and health and sports sciences

One midwifery tutor pointed out that not only do they welcome those who take gap years between school and higher education, but they also attract recruits who have taken a gap between careers, choosing midwifery as a second career.

For some reason, this group of respondents was more accepting of students who just use their gap year to save money for their studies, although healthcare subject tutors did tend to prefer students who had spent the year in voluntary or paid work broadly related to their subject.

The University of the West of England pointed out that they would not consider deferred applicants for their BSc (Hons) Physiotherapy course, while generally welcoming gap-year students.

Other issues of interest raised

Deferral

Several tutors and admissions officers commented that they need to know in advance if you intend to take a gap year. Rather than wait to be offered a place and then ask for deferred entry, they like you to make it clear on your application that you are seeking deferred entry. Alternatively, you can apply during your gap year for entry the following autumn.

Asking for deferred entry after an offer does not mean you will not get it, but it does complicate the number-crunching process for the university or college.

Sandwich courses

One tutor pointed out that if a student takes a gap year before a sandwich course, they're going to be 23 or 24 when they graduate. On the other hand, another respondent thought a gap year would help a sandwich student when they came to do their year's work placement. Another thought work experience in a gap year was wasted as the student would gain work experience in their sandwich year anyway.

Prospectuses

Most university and college prospectuses offer helpful advice on their attitudes to students who take a year off – often broken up into departmental viewpoints. Do read these before talking to admissions tutors. Three universities sent us quotes from their 2002 entry prospectuses about gap years, which may be of interest:

University College London: '10% of UCL's undergraduates elect to take a gap year between school and university. The majority use this gap year to work in industry or a profession relevant to their degree, to travel or to undertake voluntary work either in this country or overseas. All departments at UCL encourage students to do this provided that they have a structured plan and know what they want to achieve. UCAS rules allow for students to apply for deferred entry and UCL is normally happy to allow this. A gap year can bring benefits to students, not the least of which is a broadening of perspective and an increase in maturity.'

University of Strathclyde: 'The academic selectors for all courses at Strathclyde will consider applications for deferred entry (i.e. applications submitted in autumn 2001 for entry in September 2003) on their individual merits.'

The University of Warwick: 'The University of Warwick welcomes applications from candidates who wish to take a year off between school and university. It is helpful to selectors if you make clear on your UCAS form your reasons for wishing to defer your entry and how you intend to spend your time. If you plan to work in an area related to your degree subject or to travel to develop a foreign language, then this may strengthen your application.

If you definitely plan to take a year out, please indicate this on your UCAS form. You should note, though, that it is normally possible to defer entry at a later stage if you have worthwhile plans for your proposed gap year.'

The view from UCAS
Tony Higgins, Chief Executive of UCAS, gives the following advice.

'I would recommend taking time out to prospective students. However, they need to make sure that they do something constructive and worthwhile in their year, and gain useful experience and new life skills. Course-related work and voluntary experience are particularly useful, but adventurous travel, working holidays and study abroad all contribute to broadening horizons and the development of confidence and communication skills.

To those students who will return to a scientific, engineering or maths-related course, I would suggest that they spend some time looking at *their A level notes before the start of their university course. Students can find that their memory of maths and science fades quickly.*

If you are considering taking a year out, contact the admissions tutors for the courses that interest you before filling in your UCAS form. You will then be able to ascertain their views. When applying through UCAS, you will need to say what you are planning to do in your time out and what you are aiming to achieve.'

In conclusion

Higher education admissions tutors are generally very positive about students who are planning to take a year out before starting their course. Many are impressed by the extra maturity that a year out can bring. While the great majority are positive, however, individual views obviously do vary - from the highly enthusiastic, through to those who have reservations unless the time is spent in a specific way, such as gaining relevant work experience. All admissions staff do need to be assured that you will use the time constructively, and are keen to know how you hope to benefit.

While returning to study can be an initial difficulty for some, the large majority of students settle back easily. For those of you aiming at courses that involve large elements of science and maths, it is particularly important to think about how you can keep your study skills from getting too rusty. Admissions staff may be able to give advice, and recommend some reading.

If you, or perhaps your parents, were having concerns about the advisability of taking a year out, either from the point of view of being disadvantaged when making applications, or in relation to being able to cope with getting back to academic study, hopefully the responses to our survey have provided food for thought, and given you some reassurance. Far from your being disadvantaged, it is highly likely that the extra maturity and broad experience you will gain will be viewed as an asset by prospective admissions tutors.

2

Taking time out in the UK

Chapter 6
Paid employment in the UK

Paid work in the UK can be divided into:

- employment in your local area
- employment away from home
- employment related to your future career.

Paid employment in your local area

If you want the convenience and continuity of living at home during your year out, the jobs available to you will depend on what your locality can offer. It may be difficult to find work that is particularly relevant to your chosen career area. There are a number of jobs likely to be available locally, many of which do not require previous experience or qualifications. You may have to work unsocial hours or shifts, especially in the hospitality and leisure industries. Your local careers/Connexions service and Jobcentre will have details of vacancies. Look in your local paper, and ask around. Possibilities include:

- working in a hotel as a receptionist, room attendant, kitchen assistant, waiter/waitress, porter, cleaner or barperson
- working in a local pub, restaurant or fast food chain
- working in a sports or leisure centre
- cleaning homes or offices
- shop work

- working at a nursery or playscheme, or with people with special needs (your local library or council offices may have details of organisations to contact)
- working in a factory as a packer, on the production line, in the warehouse or as a delivery person
- unskilled building site work
- gardening
- office work (computer and keyboard skills may be expected)
- working in a Civil Service department or agency, or for a local council; there are sometimes temporary posts as administrative assistants or officers with such organisations which can last from a few weeks to several months
- working in a hospital or residential home as a care assistant. Contact hospitals and residential homes direct - you will find addresses in local directories such as Yellow Pages
- tele-sales and market research (this is often commission-only, so try to find out how successful, or otherwise, other people have been; it may be quite lucrative if you are good at it!)
- driving jobs.

Plan ahead, and make any speculative approaches to organisations early. It is a good idea to sign on with employment agencies, especially for temporary office, warehouse, driving, catering and cleaning work. When you sign on with an agency or make speculative applications, you will need an up-to-date CV - wordprocessed if possible, so that you can add to it later. You may find seasonal work, such as in the leisure and tourism sector in the Easter and summer holidays, or at Christmas in the retail industry. If you can, get a part-time job in one of the above areas before your time out, then try to negotiate more hours when you need them.

Paid employment away from home

Your main objective may be to get away from home for a while, or perhaps you have to leave to find the sort of job you want. In this section, you will find details of a variety of opportunities such as working on children's summer camps, in holiday parks, hotels and theme parks, in private schools, at motorway service stations, as au pairs and parents' helps and at English language schools. You could even try for a Gap Year Commission in the army.

The experience and qualifications expected for all these opportunities vary, but many of them have no set requirements. Pay also varies hugely, with the better-paid jobs usually being those for which experience or a qualification is necessary. Accommodation is often provided and, for some jobs, meals may also be included.

Work as an au pair, nanny or parent's help

Such jobs are often advertised in magazines like *The Lady* and *Nursery World*, and in local papers. There are also agencies which place au pairs with families in the UK. For many jobs you will need to be over 18. Most families will expect childcare experience or qualifications. A driving licence is often necessary.

Working in the tourism and leisure industry

There is a wide variety of work available in tourism and leisure in the UK, from working as a sports instructor at an activity centre to assisting the chef in an up-market hotel. Work may be with children or adults, or a mixture of age groups.

There are vacancies, mostly seasonal, for bar staff, general assistants, cashiers, domestic staff, shop and catering staff and office workers, as well as activity organisers and entertainers, group leaders, swimming pool attendants/lifeguards and sports instructors. Instructors need to possess qualifications in their chosen sport or activity, such as tennis, swimming, archery, fell-walking, rock climbing, windsurfing, sailing or riding.

The British Hospitality Association publishes *Your First Choice* – the directory of best employers in the tourism and hospitality industry. This publication may be available for reference in careers libraries, or you can contact the Association at Queen's House, 55/56 Lincoln's Inn Fields, London WC2A 3BH. Telephone 020 7404 7744. Details can also be found on www.etp.org.uk

Springboard UK also promotes careers in the hospitality, leisure and tourism industries. You can contact them at 3 Denmark Street, London WC2H 8LP, telephone 020 7497 8654, or visit their website at www.springboarduk.org.uk

Ardmore Language Schools

Activity specialists, EFL teachers and group leaders are recruited for Ardmore Language Schools, which are residential centres for children aged 8-17 years, located throughout southern England. Board and lodgings are provided, with wages starting from £120 per week. Applicants must be 18 years or over.

Contact: Operations Manager, Berkshire College, Burchett's Green, Maidenhead, Berks SL6 6QR.
Tel: 01628 826699. Fax: 01628 829977.
Email: mailbox@ardmore.org.uk
Website: www.ardmore.org.uk

Bourne Leisure Group Ltd

This company trades as Butlins, Haven, Warner and British Holidays, and is the biggest private leisure company in the UK. Receptionists, bar and catering staff, lifeguards and cleaners are required. Minimum age 18.

Contact: Recruitment Team UK, Bourne Leisure Group Ltd, 1 Park Lane, Hemel Hempstead, Hertfordshire HP2 4YL.

Tel: 01442 203960.

Center Parcs

Casual and temporary work is available all year round, but especially at holiday seasons.

Apply to individual Parcs or to HQ (address below).

Contact: Center Parcs Ltd, Kirklington Road, Eakring, Nottinghamshire NG22 0DZ.

Tel: 01623 872300. Fax: 01623 872399.

Choice Hotels Europe

Own, manage and franchise over 500 hotels in 13 European countries. Positions are primarily for the UK and Ireland, though guidance can be offered in identifying opportunities in Germany and France.

Experienced receptionists, chefs, waiters, waitresses and bar persons. Minimum period of work is six months, one year in front office. Good working knowledge of the English language for positions in UK/Ireland, fluent for front office work. 39h/week spread over 5 days. Salary in accordance with minimum wages regulations.

Applicants are considered all year round and everywhere in the UK (Ireland tends to be more seasonal though some opportunities are offered from September onwards).

Applicants must be over 18, customer orientated, smart and pleasant. Priority given to those with hotel qualifications and/or experience of the trade. Applications in writing (covering letter and CV).

Contact: HR Officer, Choice Hotels Europe, 112/114 Station Road, Edgware, Middlesex HA8 7BJ.

Tel: 020 8233 2001. Fax: 020 8233 2080.

Email: fbernardon@choicehotelseurope.com

Website: www.choicehotelseurope.com

HF Holidays Ltd

HF Holidays organises guided walking and special interest holidays in Britain and overseas. HF Holidays own and operate 19 country house hotels in the UK and also operate walking holidays in more than 70 destinations overseas. Walk leaders and hotel staff are required.

Walk leaders

Volunteers must be enthusiastic walkers, competent with map and compass, to guide groups of guests on week-long walking holidays throughout Europe. Travel expenses and full board accommodation are provided.

Hotel staff

For many country house hotels located throughout England, Scotland and Wales, situated in national parks and areas of outstanding natural beauty. Staff are recruited for the following positions:

Assistant management – experience essential

General assistants – combining dining room service and cleaning of public areas and guest bedrooms/bathrooms. Training will be given.

Kitchen porters – to assist in the cleanliness of the kitchen and equipment, and the preparation of vegetables and salad. Training will be given.

Assistant chefs – experience is preferable.

Chefs – practical experience required.

Head chefs – practical experience of cooking for up to 100 is essential. Rates of pay vary from £136.50 to £220 per week depending on the position; accommodation is available.

Contact: Recruitment and Training Department, HF Holidays, Redhills, Penrith, Cumbria CA11 0DT.

Tel: 01768 899988. Fax: 01768 899323

Email: rt@hfholidays.co.uk

For a leader information pack call 0208 905 9556 or visit the website.

Website: www.hfholidays.co.uk/leaders

Kingswood Centres and Camp Beaumont Summer Camps

Activity holidays organised for children aged 6 to 16. Sports instructors and counsellors are needed all year round. Activities include archery, arts and crafts, fencing, swimming, climbing, watersports, field games, computers and English language learning for overseas visitors.

Employees have the opportunity to gain National Governing Body qualifications – all food and accommodation is provided. Pay varies according to level of qualification – there are many promotion possibilities.

Contact: Kingswood Learning & Leisure Ltd, Overstrand Hall, Overstrand, Norfolk NR27 0JJ.

Tel: 01263 579771. Fax: 01263 579145.

Websites: www.kingswood.co.uk   www.campbeaumont.com
www.kingswoodlearninggrid.com

Legoland Windsor

Legoland is open from March to January, and needs staff during these months to do just about anything, including supervising the attractions, dealing with enquiries and bookings, preparing food, maintaining the grounds and buildings, cash control and selling souvenirs. Some of the jobs have a minimum age of 18, and security officers need to be over 21. There is no maximum age limit.

Apply early. Interviews (and auditions for entertainers) are held in January and February, although there are high-season vacancies which become available later. Part-time, full-time, weekend and casual work is available. People who can work throughout the season are particularly welcome.

Contact: The Human Resources Department, Legoland Windsor, Winkfield Road, Windsor SL4 4AY.

Tel: 01753 626144/145. Fax: 01753 626143

Email: jobs@legoland.co.uk

Website: www.legoland.co.uk

NST Travel Group

NTS Travel Group offers opportunities at UK Activity Centres, as well as abroad (see chapter 9). Positions available include instructors, entertainment organisers, catering staff, drivers, bar staff, cleaners etc. Two to eleven months duration.

Contact: NST Travel Group plc, Chiltern House, Bristol Avenue, Blackpool, Lancashire FY2 0FA.

Tel: 01253 503011. Fax: 01253 356955.

Email: info@nstjobs.co.uk

Website: www.nstjobs.co.uk

PGL Travel Ltd

PGL Travel is Europe's largest provider of activity courses for children, and takes on over 2,000 people to work in its centres in Britain, France and Spain. The first centres open in February and continue to operate until October, while the heaviest staffing requirements fall between May and September. Priority is given to applicants who can start in May or earlier. There are also limited vacancies just for July and August.

Vacancies exist for the following:

Instructors: Teach a variety of outdoor activities such as sailing, canoeing, rafting, surfing, safety-boat driving, rowing, swimming, pony-trekking, archery, fencing, judo, hill-walking, climbing, abseiling, caving, orienteering, assault course and raft-building. During July and August, there are limited vacancies for ball sports, racquet sports and for teachers of arts and crafts, drama and video film-making. Possession of instructor qualifications will enhance your chances of employment. PGL also runs instructor training courses.

Group leaders: Care for the children outside the main activity hours. Group leaders take responsibility for a group of children throughout their stay at the centre and act as friend, teacher, parent and counsellor. Group leaders also organise evening entertainment. Previous experience of working with children is required, minimum age is 20. During the school holidays a number of travelling courier/ group leaders are employed. Couriers accompany children on trips to various parts of Europe; a sound knowledge of at least one foreign European language is required.

Support staff: Cooks, catering staff, nurses, drivers, administrative assistants, domestic assistants, site/stores assistants, night security staff, tuck shop/bar assistants and maintenance staff. For some of these positions, previous experience is required.

Applicants need to be at least 18 years old, unless applying specifically to work in France or as a group leader for which the minimum age is 20. If you work for more than one season, you may be able to progress to a senior post.

All posts are residential; food and accommodation are provided plus pocket money ranging from £50-£80 per week, depending on start date and length of service.

In addition to the jobs mentioned above, PGL also has limited vacancies for Saturday couriers, ski resort representatives, TEFL tutors, French tutors, eastern Europe tour couriers and study visit organisers in France.

Contact: Seasonal Personnel Department, PGL Travel Ltd, Alton Court, Penyard Lane, Ross-on-Wye, Herefordshire HR9 5GL.

Tel: 01989 767833. Fax: 01989 768769

Email: personnel@pgl.co.uk   Website: www.pgl.co.uk/personnel

Warner Holidays Ltd

Holiday resorts and hotels for adults only throughout the UK require catering, bar, leisure, entertainment, cleaning, retail and receptionist staff. Competitive rates of pay, board and lodging for people over 18 years of age.

Contact: Human Resources, Warner Holidays Ltd, 1 Park Lane, Hemel Hempstead, Herts HP2 4YL.

Tel: 01442 230300. Fax: 01442 211425.

YHA

The YHA recruits over 500 temporary general hostel assistants each year. Vacancies are of varying duration, with the longest being from

February to October. There are also shorter term vacancies available. Accommodation is provided and the salary is approximately £636 per month. Responsibilities include customer service, reception duties, catering, housekeeping and general maintenance and security work. The hours average 45 per five-day week with split shifts in operation. Bank Holidays and weekend work is usual. Training is given and most new staff are able to attend a three-day induction course which includes 'Welcome Host' and 'Basic Food Hygiene'.

Applicants should ideally be over 18 with some experience of dealing with the public. Catering and clerical skills would be useful. It is possible to state a preferred location, but if you are flexible about where you would like to work it is easier for them to offer you employment. There may also be some live-out vacancies as well as more senior vacancies, but you should check what is available.

Contact: YHA, National Recruitment Department (Hostel Staff), PO Box 6030, Matlock, Derbyshire DE4 3XA.

Tel: 07626 939216 (December to June) to leave your contact details to receive information and an application form.

Email: recruitment@yha.org.uk

Website: www.yha.org.uk

Working as an assistant in independent/ boarding schools in the UK

Vacancies for assistants and assistant matrons may sometimes be available in private preparatory schools. One organisation that may have notice of vacancies is Gabbitas Educational Consultants Ltd. School-leavers can register with the Gabbitas Staff Recruitment Department for general assistant posts in preparatory schools. There are also opportunities to work in a non-teaching capacity as assistant house staff.

Contact: Gabbitas Educational Consultants Ltd, Carrington House, 126-130 Regent Street, London W1B 5EE.

Tel: 020 7734 0161. Fax: 020 7437 1764.

Email: admin@gabbitas.co.uk

Website: www.gabbitas.co.uk

The Schools Appointment Service offers the opportunity of salaried jobs in boarding schools throughout the UK. Duties include supervision, care and welfare of children aged either 7-13 years or 13-18 years. There may be opportunities to assist in the classroom, coach games or music, help with after-school activities or act as escorts. Knowledge of first aid is useful, and a driver's licence is an advantage. Board and lodging is free in term time. Jobs can last from one term to one year, or permanently. Pay varies from £280 to £500 per month. Candidates should be over 18; no qualifications are necessary.

Contact: Schools Appointment Service, 23 Peters Close, Prestwood, Bucks HP16 9ET.

Tel: 01494 863027. Fax: 01494 864122.

Website: www.annehavercroft-schoolsappointmentservices.co.uk

Profile **Victoria Credland**

Matron at a preparatory school

'I knew I wanted a 'gap year', partly because I had no idea what job I wanted after graduation, and partly because I felt I deserved a break after years of essays and exams. I wanted to do something unusual and gain experience in a different situation.

After looking into various projects/expedition organisations – which I felt were expensive – I 'fell' into my present job after applying through a schools appointment service. Initially I was looking for a PE/sports assistant job in boarding school (my degree was sports based) but I was approached to fill a 'matron' position at Papplewick Preparatory School in Ascot. I went for an interview and knew, as I drove into the school, that I would accept the job. The school looked fantastic – friendly, warm and happy.

It's a residential job and I care for 120 boys ranging from 6- to 12-years old. The job spans from waking and assisting the boys in the morning, to sorting out laundry, from booking dentist appointments and dealing with homesick boys to liaising with parents and teachers. We also read bedtime stories and play games as well as discipline the boys as and when required.

I enjoyed my job so much I agreed to stay for another academic year, by which time I had decided to apply for a PGCE course to 'convert' my degree to a teaching qualification.

By April of my second year (2001) the head matron resigned and I was asked to take the 'deputy' position, which I am currently doing. So my 'gap year' has, in fact, turned into three!

Since starting the job, I have become more patient, a better listener and adviser. I have used my imagination to a greater extent than ever before, and become more creative in my story telling skills. As deputy matron, I have increased responsibility, including for the school shop and administration.

I also help in the English department and teach swimming lessons twice a week as practice for next year on my teaching course. And as public schools have such long holidays (paid!), I've travelled extensively – Egypt, Turkey, Bavaria, Prague, Austria....

A gap year (or three) was the best decision I've made – I had time to consider my future career and find something I really love doing. Good luck with yours!'

Teaching English as a foreign language

A number of English language schools recruit teachers of English as a foreign language, to teach overseas students mainly on summer and some Easter courses. A TEFL qualification, such as the Cambridge RSA Certificate, is usually required. (See the section on TEFL qualifications in chapter 8.) Some organisations also require applicants to have a degree. Many of these schools are in places which are popular with foreign visitors, such as Bournemouth, Brighton, Cambridge, London and Oxford. TEFL jobs and courses are usually advertised in the education section of *The Guardian* on Tuesdays and in the *Times Educational Supplement* on Fridays.

EL Publications, Dilke House, Malet Street, London WC1E 7JN. Tel: 020 7255 1969, publishes *EL Gazette* at a cost of £32 per year ((£20 per half-year). This contains details of vacancies in organisations offering TEFL courses. Ring 01732 884023 to subscribe.

An information pack regarding TEFL is available from the British Council Information Centre, Bridgewater House, 58 Whitworth Street, Manchester M1 6BB Tel: 0161 957 7755. Details about British Council accredited English language schools are available from the following website: www.englishinbritain.co.uk

The following are just some English language schools which recruit teaching staff.

EJO Ltd (The Elizabeth Johnson Organisation)

Runs summer and Easter language courses mainly in the south of England. Most of the teachers employed are qualified (PGCE, BEd or TEFL) though there are some openings for graduates (preferably with a modern language degree and/or TEFL experience). There are also a few vacancies for people to organise activities and excursions. No specific qualifications are required although sporting interests are desirable.

Contact: EJO Ltd, Eagle House, Lynchborough Road, Passfield, Hampshire GU30 7SB.

Tel: 01428 751933. Fax: 01428 751944.

Website: www.ejo.co.uk

Embassy CES

Recruits staff with recognised TEFL qualification for periods of between two and nine weeks in the summer.

Contact: Embassy CES, White Rock, Hastings, East Sussex TN34 1JY.
Tel: 01424 720100.
Website: www.embassyces.com

International Community School

Summer EFL staff employed, mainly graduates with RSA Diploma.
Contact: International Community School, 4 York Terrace East,
Regent's Park, London NW1 4PT.
Tel: 020 7935 1206.

Padworth College

Contact: Padworth College, Padworth, Reading, Berkshire RG7 4NR.
Tel: 0118 983 2644.
Email: principal@padworth.co.uk
Website: www.argonet.co.uk/padworth-college

Regent Language Holidays

Contact: Regent Language Holidays, Imperial House, 40-42 Queens Road,
Brighton BN1 3XB.
Tel: 01273 718620. Fax: 01273 718621.
Email: holidays@regent.org.uk
Website: www.regent.org.uk

Victoria School of English

Employs temporary EFL staff required from June to September. Degree
plus RSA Certificate required.
Contact: Victoria School of English, 28 Graham Terrace,
Sloane Square, London SW1W 8JH.
Tel: 020 7730 1333.
Website: www.victoriaschool.co.uk

The Army Gap Year Commissions Scheme

Each year about 70 young men and women, waiting to go to
university, are offered Gap Year Commissions in the Army. They serve
from four to eighteen months as officers in regular units, either in
the UK or abroad, and have no further liability. A salary of £10,267 is
paid on appointment and rises to £11,717 after nine months.
Applicants must have reached the age of 18 years and be under 20
years on the day of commissioning, and must have already gained a
university place. The closing date for applications is 31 August.
Contact: Tel: 0345 300111.

A student who took part in the scheme wrote that it was:

> 'Not a recruiting effort, only a public relations exercise, i.e. to disseminate a sympathetic attitude to the Army in university and beyond. After only a month's very rushed training, I was in Germany and soon fulfilling a normal junior officer's job, i.e. administering a troop of three tanks and the crew of 11 men besides myself. Although it is not the life for me, I enjoyed the responsibility and the complete break from academic pursuits. The scheme is financially very rewarding, valuable in terms of experiences, and entails no commitment to the Army during, or after, university. Having said that, the experience I gained will stand me in very good stead in whatever employment I do.'

Employment related to your future career

Our survey of employers in chapter 4 shows that they rate relevant paid work experience in a gap year very highly. This type of opportunity may be difficult to find - so be prepared to start applying early and to be persistent! If you do manage to find a placement prior to your higher education, the employer may well offer you vacation work during your course, which, in turn, could eventually lead to permanent employment.

To impress employers, emphasise any keyboard, computing and language skills you have, as well as relevant academic qualifications and personal qualities. Even a job as temporary office junior or production worker will help to give you an understanding of the industry concerned, and will make your CV stand out from those with no relevant experience at all, when looking for permanent work later. If you can't get paid work in your chosen career area during your year out, a short spell of unpaid work experience or work shadowing is also likely to impress, especially if you have to use your initiative to gain such an opportunity.

Some organisations, such as The Year in Industry, IBM and Towers Perrin, recruit students who want to gain experience in industry during their year out. You will find their details below.

The Andersen Scholarship Programme

The programme is a 35-week placement comprising paid training and work, followed by academic sponsorship whilst at university and further paid vacation work. It will be in one of the specialist divisions – corporate tax consulting, assurance risk consulting, global corporate finance or business consulting. Around 75 places are available each year across the UK. Students receive a competitive salary during the course of the gap placement, a travel bursary of £1500 and an annual academic sponsorship of £1500 per year of an undergraduate degree.

Candidates should have a strong interest in pursuing a career in business and finance, and should have predicted As and Bs at A level, plus GCSE maths at grade A.

Contact: Andersen, 180 The Strand, London WC2R 1BL.

Tel: 0500 592 800.

Email: ukcareers@andersen.com

Website: www.andersen.com/ukcareers

IBM student programmes

IBM UK offer a number of student programmes, all of which offer a salary while on placement. Placements may be available at one of 25 IBM locations across the UK and Ireland.

The Pre-University Employment Scheme lasts for twelve months and offers structured training and work experience, both in technical and non-technical areas. While those planning to study maths and sciences are obvious candidates, numerate students from any discipline may apply. Students must have predicted AAB grades (340 new UCAS tariff points) at A level, plus GCSE grades A-C in maths and English. Computer experience is not essential for every position. A deferred place at university must be secured.

The Industrial Trainee Placement Scheme is for students who are studying for a degree, having attained at least 220 A level points, plus GCSE grades A-C in maths and English. The placement lasts twelve months.

There is an integrated three-year degree scheme, based at Portsmouth University. Students must have at least 300 A level points, plus maths and English GCSEs.

Contact: Student Recruitment, F2Q, IBM United Kingdom Ltd,
PO Box 41, North Harbour, Portsmouth PO6 3AU.
Recruitment hotline: 023 9256 4104

Website: www.student_pgms@uk.ibm.com

KPMG

The gap programme is designed to give students an insight into a professional services firm. It runs for either a six-month or a nine-month period and is offered in offices throughout the country. Students will work at a client's office or from the KPMG office, as a member of a team; they will receive £12,500 (to be revised). Students should be aiming for at least 240 UCAS points, having already attained a grade A in GCSE maths.

Contact: KPMG, 1 Puddle Dock, London EC4V 3PD.
Tel: 0500 664665. Fax: 0207 311 2753.
Email: Sara.Hutchinson@kpmg.co.uk
Website: www.kpmgcareers.co.uk

PricewaterhouseCoopers

PricewaterhouseCoopers offers an insight into the financial world through its gap-year programme. The programme offers a competitive salary and lasts six months (October to March). It is for those with a strong academic record who are capable of achieving good A level results. To apply, or read more about the programme:

Tel: 0808 100 1500

Website: www.pwcglobal.com/uk/bridges

Towers Perrin

Towers Perrin is an international firm of consulting actuaries and management consultants. It offers gap-year employment from 1 September until mid-May of the following year to students wishing to take a year out between study at 18 and higher education.

Gap year students will work in the Property Casualty unit (General Insurance) or Employee Benefits Services unit, both of which are actuarial units. The work will appeal to students with a strong interest in maths and computing. Applicants should expect to gain a high grade at A level maths and at least two other high grade A levels, or equivalent.

Towers Perrin will provide valuable hands-on experience working in an actuarial consultancy together with in-depth computer training. The job is rewarding both financially and intellectually. The positions are based in London, Newbury or St Albans.

Interested students should apply in October/November of their final year of A levels/Advanced GNVQ/BTEC/Highers etc.

Contact: Towers Perrin, Castlewood House, 77-91 New Oxford Street, London WC1A 1PX.

Email: act-grades@towers.com

Website: www.towers.com

Profile **Alexi Pilavakis**

Work in the financial sector with Towers Perrin

'Whether or not to take a gap year is one of the most thought-provoking decisions you have to make. It was after much deliberation that I finally decided not to take one. I'd get out of the rhythm of work. I was looking forward to going straight to university and studying a new subject. And yet here I am, rather ironically, currently on a gap year.

So, what changed my mind? In short, my first-choice university, which offered me a place for deferred entry only. Having accepted their offer, the question then was how to occupy myself for a little over a year.

With a career in the financial sector in mind, I applied to several firms ranging from banking to chartered accountancy. After several interviews and assessment days, invaluable experiences in themselves, I accepted an offer from an internationally renowned actuarial consultancy, Towers Perrin.

I joined Towers Perrin in September as an analyst in the Employee Benefits Services department of one of their six UK-based offices. EBS focuses on designing and advising on the pension schemes and other employee benefits offered by large multinational companies. I was immediately made to feel part of a team of highly motivated and dedicated people.

As a gap year analyst, I attended the same training courses and induction sessions as the graduate recruits. These also provided excellent opportunities to meet gap-year students and staff from the other offices.

Workflow meetings, your own personal mentor and performance assessments, are all ways of ensuring that you get the most out of your time with the firm. As a result, I have been involved with varied and challenging projects. These have included creating and managing databases, preparing client presentations, carrying out new business research, designing spreadsheets and performing benefit calculations.

In turn, I have improved my time-management and organisational skills - essential when you have several assignments to complete with deadlines. Working alongside experienced professionals has made me more self-confident and responsible. I have made new friends and contacts and earned some financial independence. And I've gained invaluable work experience and a clearer career perspective.

For someone who took 'a year off' not fully convinced of its potential benefits, I can now look back, almost 'a year on', and honestly say that a gap year is an excellent way of improving and motivating yourself. I now look forward to starting university fresh from ten months of work and three months of travel.'

The Year in Industry

This year about 800 young people will get their first taste of industry through The Year in Industry scheme; on past results, around 90% will return to industry after graduation, equipped with the experience and skills widely valued by employers.

The scheme is seen by many employers as a way of tapping into the limited pool of talented young people, especially in areas such as science, engineering and information technology. Over 250 companies regularly take part - from 'blue chip' multinationals to small/medium-sized enterprises. Placements span a wide range of industries - from biotechnology to transport, from research and consultancy to energy and utilities and project work is varied and wide-ranging.

Whatever the differences between placements, there is always a common thread; the work is challenging and carries responsibility; students are set objectives and have to manage themselves, their time and their projects in order to achieve results. Students build their teamworking and communication skills as well as their understanding of business and industry, all of which will have a lasting impact on their future career.

The Year in Industry is available nationwide and is open to any student interested in a career in industry, whatever degree course they are taking; the majority of placements are for students considering degrees in engineering, science and technology - a reflection of companies' shortage skills. Current minimum salary is £150 per week. The package includes 'off the job' training to develop interpersonal skills and business awareness. Applications should be made as early as possible in the final year of A levels/Highers/vocational A levels etc.

Contact: The Year in Industry National Director, University of Manchester, Simon Building, Oxford Road, Manchester M13 9PL.

Email: enquiries@yini.org.uk   Website: www.yini.org.uk

The Year in Industry - just some experiences

Sebastian Pearce jetted around Europe as part of his Year in Industry with GKN Auto Structures. He investigated the supply chain for the new Transit being made in Turkey. By bringing about a few changes, including in the way parts were packaged, Sebastian was able to save the organisation over £51,000.

Stephanie Rose McGovern worked for Black & Decker. She was faced with a capacity problem - the company couldn't keep up with the increased demand for their garden vacuum/blower in the USA. Stephanie successfully managed to reduce cycle time and runout which will result in a total saving of more than £150,000!

Alex Scordellis worked with a team at Snell & Wilcox to produce a device for introducing stills, clips and promos straight into production switchers – this is useful for live news or sports production applications. The 'FlexiCache' was launched at an exhibition in Las Vegas in April 2001 and is expected to generate a revenue stream of $5 – 6 million in its first year!

Chris Vessey worked at KP Foods to minimise the landfill costs from the production of a snack food. He had to meet quality and safety requirements in order to recycle some of the waste products. The final result of extensive research and tests were huge cost savings and reduced environmental impact.

Aoife Doran spent her Year in Industry working for Avecia, a large speciality chemical manufacturer. She introduced a new bio-toxicity test in one of the company's environmental laboratories and then trained others to use it. By testing on-site, £400 per sample is saved. It has also increased turnover time and the volume of business for the lab.

Matthew James Justin Storey contributed greatly to the work of a team at Magnox Electric plc to help the Wylfa Nuclear Power Station in North Wales return to safe service. The station, capable of producing 1000 MW of electricity, had been shut down for fifteen months. Every day that the station was down represented a cost of £440,000!

Sponsorship

If you are lucky enough to have found a company to sponsor your higher education, they may be willing to offer you gap-year employment first, and also vacation work throughout your course. See the bibliography in Part 5 for sources of information about sponsorship.

Chapter 7
Voluntary work in the UK

Voluntary work in the UK can be as basic as spending your time doing gardening and shopping for your elderly neighbours, or working in your community playgroup or pre-school. But most people choose to find an opportunity with a voluntary organisation, which has aims and values that they wish to support. This is a more structured way of volunteering, and usually offers back-up and training where necessary, and often some help with expenses and pocket money.

Organisations vary considerably in size, ethos, resources and the type of voluntary work available. Many have a basis in religious principles.

Most opportunities can be divided into two groups:

- community work - helping disadvantaged children, young adults with special needs, families or elderly people, as carers and helpers, through fundraising or by practical work such as providing and maintaining facilities

- environmental and conservation work - often outdoors, conserving wildlife, countryside or historic buildings and artefacts through practical, manual work or by scientific or historical research.

There are also opportunities for volunteers to help on the administrative and clerical side of some organisations.

Some schemes will provide accommodation - be it a tent, a hostel or a bedsit. Some will offer token financial help in the way of living or travel expenses, while others will require you to pay your way, and possibly make a donation. Make sure you know exactly what the arrangements are before you undertake a placement. Where possible, we have included this sort of information in the entries below.

The length of a placement can also vary considerably - anything from a weekend to two years, so you need to decide whether you want to spend all your time out on one scheme, or whether to combine it with paid work, study or travel.

Think carefully about what you hope to gain from a period of voluntary work, as well as what you have to give. Do some research into any schemes, which appeal to you, and be sure that you believe in and agree with the organisation's objectives. Make sure the organisation offers whatever preparation and support you think you will require.

Previous experience is usually not required as volunteers generally work with, or are guided by, experienced staff.

The minimum age for voluntary projects is often 18 but, in some cases, organisations will accept 16- or 17-year olds. Some organisations set an upper age limit of, say, 25, 30 or 35.

To help you to find the right scheme for you, we have coded the entries below as follows:

C = conservation and environmental work
S = social projects and community work
W = work camps - often with people from overseas working on a practical project for a short period of time.

Most volunteer placements require no experience or qualifications, but there are occasions when practical or scientific skills are particularly useful.

An appropriate voluntary work placement will almost certainly result in your gaining maturity, confidence, communication, teamwork and leadership skills. You will find out a lot about yourself and how you relate to other people.

Organisations which offer information on volunteering opportunities

National Association of Volunteer Bureaux

There are more than 400 volunteer bureaux throughout England. Bureaux are 'signposting agencies' for volunteers and provide information about a wide range of local opportunities. They give advice and guidance on how prospective volunteers can use their time and they find people specific opportunities by referring them to a statutory agency (for example, a social services department), voluntary organisation or informal volunteer group. Some bureaux also recruit volunteers for projects they have initiated themselves. Check out your local volunteer bureau by looking in the telephone directory under Volunteer Bureaux or Council for Voluntary Service, or contact your local Citizens' Advice Bureau or local council.

Contact: National Association of Volunteer Bureaux, New Oxford House, Waterloo Street, Birmingham B2 5UG.

Tel: 0121 633 4555. Fax: 0121 633 4043.

Email: info@navb.org.uk

Website: www.navb.org.uk

The National Centre for Volunteering

Publishes a series of factsheets including ones on finding voluntary work and volunteering overseas. They also have a website with information on volunteer issues.

Contact: The National Centre for Volunteering, Regents Wharf, 8 All Saints Street, London N1 9RL.

Tel: 020 7520 8900.

Email: information@thecentre.org.uk

Website: www.volunteering.org.uk

The National Youth Agency (NYA)

The NYA publishes an annual newspaper called *Volunteer Action* which gives details of voluntary work opportunities in the UK and overseas. Copies are free to young people, £1.00 to others.

The NYA website also has information about voluntary work opportunities for young people in the Community Action section of the site.

Contact: The National Youth Agency, 17-23 Albion Street, Leicester LE1 6GD.

Tel: 0116 285 3792. Fax: 0116 285 3777.

Email: info@nya.org.uk

Website: www.nya.org.uk

Voluntary Service Belfast (VSB)

VSB operates the largest volunteer bureau for the city of Belfast, and arranges voluntary work opportunities on its own projects and for 400 other user agencies. This involves work with older people, the disabled, children and young people. The work includes youth work, befriending, research projects, advice work, counselling, arts and crafts, conservation and decorating. Applicants must be over 16 and recruitment is ongoing throughout the year.

VSB is also responsible for the Belfast Cares Initiative which is a programme designed to promote employer supported volunteering by encouraging teams to take up a challenge for a community group.

Contact: Volunteer Centre, Voluntary Service Belfast, 70-72 Lisburn Road, Belfast BT9 6AF.
Tel: 028 9020 0850. Fax: 028 9020 0860.
Email: info@vsb.org.uk
Website: www.vsb.org.uk

Wales Council for Voluntary Action (WCVA)

WCVA provides information about voluntary work opportunities in Wales. Contact WCVA for a copy of *A Short Guide to Voluntary Work Opportunities in Wales*, which contains information about voluntary organisations throughout Wales, including addresses and contact names.

Contact: Volunteering Team, Wales Council for Voluntary Action, Baltic House, Mount Stuart Square, Cardiff CF10 5FH.
Tel: 029 2043 1727. Fax: 029 2043 1701.
Email: enquiries@wcva.org.uk
Website: www.volunteering-wales.net

Worldwide Volunteering for Young People

Worldwide Volunteering for Young People is a registered charity offering a computer database of volunteering opportunities in the UK and worldwide for 16 to 25 year-olds. It contains details of over 250,000 placements with 810 organisations lasting anything from one week to a year. The volunteer enters their own details and criteria onto the system, and receives a list of placements or projects, which match those criteria. It is available in many schools, universities, careers services etc - so ask locally, or you can apply to the address below for a questionnaire.

Contact: Worldwide Volunteering, Higher Orchard, Sandford Orcas, Sherborne, Dorset DT9 4RP.
Tel/fax: 01963 220036.
Email: yfb@worldvol.co.uk
Website: www.worldwidevolunteering.org.uk

Young Scot

Young Scot provides young people aged 12-26 with information, ideas and incentives that can enable them to make informed decisions, turn their own ideas into action and take advantage of opportunities available to young people throughout Europe. It provides a youth information and opportunities package, which includes *The Information Book* and The Euro 26 Discount Card.

Contact: Young Scot, Head Office, Roseberry House, 9 Haymarket Terrace, Edinburgh EH12 5EZ.

Tel: 0131 313 2488. Fax: 0131 313 6800.

Email: info@youngscot.org

Website: www.youngscot.org

Organisations offering voluntary work opportunities

ATD Fourth World   S/W

ATD works with the poorest and most disadvantaged in society, and offers a three-month introductory programme and workcamps in the UK (minimum length of service is two weeks). For more details see their entry in chapter 10.

BTCV   C

BTCV is the UK's largest practical conservation charity supporting the activities of over 130,000 volunteers in positive steps to improve the environment. Over 600 UK and international conservation holidays take place every day of the year throughout England, Wales, Scotland and Northern Ireland and in countries as far afield as the USA and Japan. Prices start from £45 per week including food and accommodation. The accommodation can vary to suit everyone's needs and pocket from a village hall to a fully-catered youth hostel.

Projects range from managing woodlands for wildlife, improving access to the countryside and reviving traditional skills such as dry-stone walling and coppicing. Volunteers must be 16 and over. No experience is required. You do, however, need to be physically fit and have plenty of enthusiasm.

BTCV's network of over 165 offices relies on the help of volunteers giving up at least three months of their time. Volunteers receive full training and support in organising and setting up environmental projects, fundraising, publicity and administration of BTCV offices. Voluntary work with BTCV is an excellent stepping stone to a career in conservation.

BTCV also has over 2500 local groups working most weekends and numerous mid-week projects throughout the country. In addition, BTCV organises over 500 training courses every year covering basic conservation skills to project management, leadership and photography.

Contact: BTCV Customer Call Centre, BTCV, 36 St Mary's Street, Wallingford, Oxfordshire OX10 0EU.

Tel: 01491 821600. Fax: 01491 839646.

Email: information@btcv.org

Website: www.btcv.org

The Camphill Village Trust   S

The Trust aims to help people with a wide range of difficulties, including learning disabilities and mental illness, to gain more independence and to lead more fulfilling lives. Many of the residents come to the Trust for assessment and rehabilitation before moving to another community. Volunteers live communally with the residents and the more permanent co-workers. The Trust runs villages, where the residents work on the land or in workshops.

Volunteers should be at least 20 and the minimum length of service is six months, but preferably one year. Board, lodging and pocket money are provided. Applications are received throughout the year.

Contact: Coordinator, Camphill Village Trust, Delrow House, Hilfield Lane, Aldenham, Watford, Hertfordshire WD25 8DJ.

Tel: 01923 856006.

Email: email@delrow.newnet.co.uk

Profile   Birte Sina

A year in Camphill

'Just one year ago, I was in the same situation as many British students - including you - might be right now: not sure what kind of course to choose at university; needing to go far away from home and to get some more experiences before university; wanting to do something totally different from studying! So I thought about volunteering. A friend of mine told me about the work experience in a Camphill community, and right away I was interested.

In Camphill, people live a community life, which means people with special needs and co-workers of all ages live together. There are Camphill places all over the world for disabled children, adolescents and adults, who join school or college courses or live in villages and do different crafts, or work on farms.

The young co-workers work in the houses and in the workshops and, of course, they assist the disabled people, which means helping to organise their weekends, sharing meals together and offering evening activities. I enjoy the idea of being creative and responsible for my own ideas.

Now is the end of my time in Camphill, and I am sure that the decision to go to Camphill was the right one. Next to improving my English, I have learned a lot about community life, about living with people with disabilities and, last of all, about myself!'

Careforce   S

Careforce serves evangelical churches and organisations, throughout the UK and the Republic of Ireland, by placing Christian volunteers (aged 18-25) where their help is most needed. Careforce enables volunteers to offer themselves to serve God in an area of need and to share fully in the life of a Christian community.

Placements include serving with local churches, youth and schools work, evangelistic outreach, and helping people who are homeless, elderly, have drug/alcohol-related problems, have a physical disability or learning difficulties, or are from families facing difficulties.

All Careforce volunteers are provided with their board and lodging plus weekly pocket money. The Careforce year begins in September and lasts for ten to twelve months with volunteers being placed according to their gifts, skills, experience and abilities. In September 2000, Careforce placed 123 volunteers.

Interviews, for placements starting the following September, are held from January through to August.

Contact: Ian Prior, Careforce, 35 Elm Road, New Malden, Surrey KT3 3HB.
Tel: 020 8942 3331. Fax: 020 8942 3331
Email: enquiry@careforce.co.uk
Website: www.careforce.co.uk

Cathedral Camps   C/W

Volunteers aged 16-30 are needed from the last week in July to early September to work at 26 cathedrals and churches helping with conservation, restoration and maintenance. Each camp lasts one week and you are asked to contribute towards board and lodging.

Contact: Cathedral Camps, 16 Glebe Avenue, Flitwick, Bedfordshire MK45 1HS.
Tel: 01525 716237.
Email: admin@cathedralcamps.org.uk
Website: www.cathedralcamps.org.uk

Church Mission Society (CMS) S

Britain 'Make a difference' placements are for those in the 18-30-age range, and provide opportunities for young people to gain experience of a part of Britain that is culturally different from what they are used to. Placements are for six to eighteen months and are based in a church or social outreach programme. CMS provides the cost of training and pays living expenses and pocket money, but participants are responsible for other costs.

Contact: The Experience Programmes Adviser, Partnership House, CMS, 157 Waterloo Road, London SE1 8UU.

Tel: 020 7928 8681. Fax: 020 7401 3215.

Email: kathy.tyson@cms-uk.org

Website: www.cms-uk.org

The Commonwealth Institute C/S

The Commonwealth Institute offers voluntary work opportunities relating to educational programmes, the leisure industry, exhibitions and the arts. There are no age restrictions.

Contact (sending CV and covering letter): The Personnel Department, The Commonwealth Institute, 230 Kensington High Street, London W8 6NQ.

Tel: 020 7603 4535.

Website: www.commonwealth.org

The Corrymeela Community C/W

Corrymeela is an ecumenical community committed to the work of peace and reconciliation in Ireland and beyond. Volunteers on the Serve and Learn programme work at the Community's centre on the North Antrim coast at Ballycastle. They undertake domestic and manual work in running the centre as well as being directly involved with the wide variety of groups that use the centre.

A balance is sought of young adults, aged 18-30, from Ireland and overseas who are willing to live in a demanding community setting, and are able to relate to a wide range of people from different backgrounds. The Community seeks people who can handle responsibility and are willing to be flexible. Applicants who have an active Christian commitment to the work of reconciliation are preferred.

12 volunteers are required for one-year positions beginning in September and two volunteers are needed for six months beginning in March. There are also summer voluntary programmes lasting two weeks. Those interested should apply by the end of February for the one-year positions, by the end of October/November for the six-months positions and by the end of April for the summer positions.

Room and board are provided for volunteers and those who volunteer for six months or a year are paid £30 a week pocket money.

Contact: Volunteer Coordinator, Corrymeela Community, 5 Drumaroan Road, Ballycastle, County Antrim BT54 6QU.

Tel: 028 2076 2626.

Email: ballycastle@corrymeela.org

Website: www.corrymeela.org

Council for British Archaeology   C

Information about excavations, and other archaeological fieldwork, can be obtained from the Council for British Archaeology. Individual membership of the Council costs £24 within the UK and includes a magazine, *British Archaeology*, published six times a year with a section giving details of many projects throughout Britain. Members also automatically belong to CBA Regional Groups, which can provide more detailed information on projects in their area. It is possible to subscribe to the magazine without joining the Council for £19 a year. It is then necessary to write to the director of the project(s) which interest(s) you. Some form of subsistence pay is sometimes provided; previous experience is not necessarily required.

Contact: The Council for British Archaeology, Bowes Morrell House, 111 Walmgate, York Y01 9WA.

Tel: 01904 671417. Fax: 01904 671384.

Email: info@britarch.ac.uk

Website: www.britarch.ac.uk

CSV   S

UK charity CSV offers the chance to do something positive in a gap year, whatever your grades. If you are aged 16-35 CSV will send you where your help is needed, to benefit local communities throughout the UK as a full-time volunteer.

800 projects include:

- working with homeless people
- assisting disabled students to attend university
- supporting young people leaving care.

Whether you plan a break from education or unexpectedly have time on your hands, CSV guarantees placements for everyone wanting to work away from home for up to a year. No previous experience or specific qualifications are required.

Whatever your planned career, you'll gain skills and experience which look good on your CV and UCAS form, and the reward of helping other people. For students studying areas such as medicine, social work or psychology, CSV can provide the practical experience and challenges, which cannot be taught in a lecture theatre.

CSV costs you nothing but your time. Projects are from four to twelve months depending on what time you have to spare. Each of the 3000 volunteers receives free accommodation, travel expenses, food and a weekly allowance of £27. Volunteers are also provided with an induction programme, on-the-job support and back-up from CSV. For more information and to apply online see their website.

Contact: CSV, 237 Pentonville Road, London N1 9NJ.

Tel: freephone 0800 374991.

Website: www.csv.org.uk

Profile Helen Claire Jones
Voluntary work with CSV at Merthyr Independence

'My name is Claire Jones and I'm not a saint. I don't wear Laura Ashley dresses and I can't remember the last time I went to church. I am also a volunteer. In general volunteers have a poor public image - either you're the unwanted do-gooder or else the religious missionary. In reality the volunteers I have met through CSV have been ordinary young people lending a hand, helping those who need it whether they be young, old, disabled or just damaged by life.

I took my year out simply because I couldn't decide what to do - I didn't feel ready for university, and anyway, I'd changed my mind as to what course to do. Another UCAS rotation later and I'm ready and enthusiastic about my degree course in Media Production - Hollywood beckons.

So why choose CSV?

If you want fabulous riches, glamorous surroundings and an easy ride - then don't! But if you're the kind of person who wants a challenge, a chance to prove yourself and are willing to be flexible and just a teeny bit 'selfless' for a while then GO FOR IT!

Here at Merthyr Independence I am part of a three-person volunteer team who aid young people who have been in care and are living independently for the first time. I help with day-to-day tasks like shopping, cooking, planning and housework, which the young people may never have done before. I'm also there to give advice and support when the young people need it. If they want to get involved with education, training or leisure activities as well as looking for work, then I'll give them a hand with that. Every day presents new challenges, and yes, new problems. But my six-month placement has given me the confidence and training to deal with anything (just don't ask me to cook). I've valued the support of the staff who supervise me as well as meeting other CSV volunteers in Merthyr.

I am near the end of my placement now and student squalor beckons! My life will surely take me far away from Merthyr Tydfil but I will never forget what I learnt here.'

Earthwatch   C

Earthwatch uses paying volunteers to help scientists working on projects in the UK and abroad. For details see the Earthwatch entry in chapter 10.

Ffestinog Railway Company   C

Volunteers are required to help in the maintenance and running of this famous narrow-gauge railway. A wide variety of work is possible. This can mean working in booking offices, guards' vans, buffet cars, shops, café and small sales outlets; cleaning locomotives; working on the footplate and driving; turning, welding, machining, steam-fitting, sheet-metal work, joinery, upholstery and paint work. Other work includes the repair of fences, bridges, culverts and dry-stone walling.

Volunteers also help in maintaining the historic buildings, parks and gardens in which the railway runs. Training is given where necessary. Working for the Ffestinog Railway Company qualifies under the Duke of Edinburgh's Award Scheme. Volunteers should be aged 16 and over unless they are in a supervised party. All volunteers must be physically fit. Limited self-catering hostel accommodation is available for regular volunteers, for which a small charge is made. Camping space and lists of local accommodation are also available.

Contact: The Volunteer Resource Officer, Ffestinog Railway Company, Harbour Station, Porthmadog, Gwynedd LL49 9NF.

Tel: 01766 516040. Fax: 01766 514576.

Email: tricia.doyle@festrail.co.uk

Website: www.festrail.co.uk

Groundwork   S/C

Groundwork is a federation of more than 40 local Trusts in England, Wales and Northern Ireland, working with partners in deprived neighbourhoods to deliver thousands of projects which improve the quality of the local environment, the lives of local people and the profitability of local businesses.

If you would like to get involved contact Groundwork at the address on the next page.

Contact: Groundwork UK, 85-87 Cornwall Street, Birmingham B3 3BY.
Tel: 0121 236 8565. Fax: 0121 236 7356.
Email: info@groundwork.org.uk
Website: www.groundwork.org.uk

The Guide Association   S

Volunteers are taken on for administrative and domestic duties at Guide Centres both in the UK and abroad. Volunteers should hold membership of an organisation affiliated to the World Association of Girl Guides and Girl Scouts and be 18 or over. Length of service varies from Centre to Centre. The number of vacancies is limited, and applications should be made as far in advance as possible. Accommodation and level of remuneration depend upon the Centre. The volunteer generally pays travelling expenses.

Contact: The Guide Association, 17-19 Buckingham Palace Road, London SW1W 0PT.
Tel: 020 7834 6242.
Website: www.guides.org.uk

Ironbridge Gorge Museum Trust   C

The Trust was established in 1967 to conserve, restore and interpret the rich industrial heritage of the Gorge, the birthplace of the Industrial Revolution. The Museum comprises seven main sites and has been created around a unique series of industrial monuments, concentrated on the pottery and iron industries, and spreads over some six square miles.

Volunteers are needed to work on various sites, doing a variety of tasks. These include site maintenance and conservation, costume making and repair, documentation, research, theatre, exhibit demonstration and interpretation, and work with a junior volunteer group.

In return the volunteers receive luncheon vouchers, free entry to all the Gorge museums, insurance, costumes and tools if necessary. Accommodation is not available but there are youth hostels and campsites nearby.

Contact: Lisa Wood, Operations Manager, Blists Hill Victorian Town, Ironbridge Gorge Museum Trust, The Wharfage, Ironbridge, Telford, Shropshire TF8 7AW.
Tel: 01952 583003. Fax: 01952 588016.
Email: blistshill@ironbridge.org.uk
Website: www.ironbridge.co.uk

Jesuit Volunteer Communities (JVC) Britain   S

JVC offers young adults (18-35) a year of living in lay communities while working in an area of social need. Volunteers live in communities of five or six, in inner city areas of Birmingham, Glasgow, Liverpool and Manchester, and work in a variety of placements organised by JVC and other agencies. Placements include working with people who are homeless, those with mental health problems, learning difficulties and victims of crime. Volunteers receive rent, bill and food allowances and pocket money.

JVC offers a Development Programme, which all volunteers attend. The JVC year begins in August with a six-day orientation and introduction. The programme continues with a weekend in November on community, a weekend in February on social justice, a communal retreat in May, and finishes with evaluation in mid-August.

Volunteers should be able to commit themselves to one year of service and need to have a wish to live in a community, a desire to live simply, a willingness to explore personal and Christian spirituality (a means of reflection on experience, life and social justice) and a commitment to work for justice.

Contact: Kate Goodrich/Chris Hogg, JVC Britain, 23 New Mount Street, Manchester M4 4DE.

Tel: 0161 832 6888. Fax: 0161 832 6958.

Email: staff@jvc.u-net.com

Website: www.jesuitvolunteers-uk.org

L'Arche   S

L'Arche is a registered charity, and L'Arche communities are places where people with and without learning disabilities live together. Volunteers are needed to work in a community with people with learning disabilities. The organisation views the spiritual life of working together as being as important as material welfare.

Assistants need to be at least 18. Craft skills are useful for workshops and for domestic duties. Free board and lodging are provided, plus pocket money. Most communities ask volunteers to stay for six months, but one year is preferable. Many assistants stay on for between one and two years.

Contact (enclosing SAE): L'Arche, 10 Briggate, Silsden, Keighley, West Yorkshire BD20 9JT.

Tel: 01535 656186. Fax: 01535 656426.

Email: info@larche.org.uk

Website: www.larche.org.uk

Leonard Cheshire   S

This organisation offers voluntary work opportunities, mainly helping with the care of adults with severe physical disabilities. Volunteers should be over 18 and have a genuine concern for the disabled. Previous experience is an advantage, but not essential. A good knowledge of the English language and communication skills are needed.

The minimum length of service is two months, but few vacancies are for less than three months. Immediate vacancies are rare, so apply early leaving time for a vacancy to arise. Applicants need to state the dates they can offer and how long they are available for. About 70-80 volunteers are recruited each year.

Board and accommodation (sometimes sharing) are provided in a home, with pocket money. The volunteer pays travel expenses. Placements are organised through GAP (see chapter 10).

Contact: Information Officer, Leonard Cheshire, 30 Millbank, London SW1P 4QD.

Tel: 020 7802 8200. Fax: 020 7802 8250.

Website: www.leonard-cheshire.org

Marine Conservation Society   C

Can sometimes offer voluntary work at the offices in Ross-on-Wye, doing routine office tasks and maintaining computer databases. Volunteers can develop their interest in marine conservation through access to the Society's resources and contact with staff. The Society can also offer help in setting up a local voluntary group or organising fundraising and publicity activities.

Student placements may be available where the university or college provides financial support.

Contact: Marine Conservation Society, 9 Gloucester Road, Ross-on-Wye, Herefordshire HR9 5BU

Tel: 01989 566017. Fax: 01980 567815

Email: info@mcsuk.org

Website: www.mcsuk.org

The National Trust Long Term Volunteering   C

Between education and work, on a university or college sandwich course, or between jobs, there are dozens of volunteer placements available throughout England, Wales and Northern Ireland that may suit you. Placements vary from working alongside a warden or forester with countryside management, to assisting house staff with running and conserving historic buildings. You could also be involved in gardening, archaeology, education or promotion.

The scheme is for anyone over 18 years of age who can offer the Trust 21 hours or more a week, for periods ranging from three months to a year. They'll aim to integrate your interests and expertise with their own needs in what almost always proves to be a worthwhile partnership. They won't expect you to be qualified or trained before starting; enthusiasm, common sense and adaptability are often as important as experience or qualifications. Self-catering accommodation is available in most regions. Applicants are accepted all year round.

The National Trust Working Holidays   C

The National Trust runs a series of more than 450 voluntary working holidays in England, Wales and Northern Ireland throughout the year. The work usually consists of outdoor conservation schemes on the Trust's many beautiful properties, often in remote places. Projects range from constructing dry-stone walls, maintaining woodland pathways to surveying wild flowers and setting up a jazz festival. The work is hard, but very rewarding.

Working Holidays can be from two to seven days and there are usually about 12 people per group. Volunteers pay from £51 a week towards the cost of food and accommodation. The accommodation ranges from cottages and farmhouses to converted stable blocks. Volunteers should be 17 or over, fit, enthusiastic and willing to be part of a team. An experienced leader and/or a Trust Warden Naturalist supervises all practical work and instruction. Approximately 3500 people are recruited annually. There is no closing date for applications but since women tend to apply earlier the places for women get filled very quickly. Working on the projects qualifies under the Duke of Edinburgh's Award Scheme. Volunteers completing 40 hours of voluntary work receive free access to National Trust properties for a year.

Contact: The National Trust, PO Box 84, Cirencester GL7 1ZP.

Tel: 01285 651818.

Website: www.nationaltrust.org.uk/volunteers

Ockenden International   S

Volunteers aged 18 plus are required to work in a residential care home in Camberley, Surrey. Residents include people with severe learning difficulties or physical disabilities, as well as Vietnamese and Cambodian orphans. Tasks include domestic and driving work, as well as helping residents to develop their abilities and confidence. Placements are for a minimum of six months, usually a year. A volunteer support worker allowance of £35 per week is paid, on top of free board and lodging. Volunteers are expected to work shifts averaging a 40-hour week, and are allowed holidays.

Contact: Personnel Officer, Ockenden International, Kilmore House, Camberley, Surrey GU15 1DQ.

Tel: 01276 709709. Fax: 01276 709707.

Email: ov@ockenden.org.uk

Website: www.ockenden.org.uk

Quaker Voluntary Action (QVA)   S/W/C

QVA provides short-term placements in the UK and abroad, including community arts work in Belfast. See chapter 10 for more details.

The Royal Society for the Protection of Birds (RSPB)   C

The RSPB has places for voluntary wardens on RSPB nature reserves in Britain, assisting the permanent warden, carrying out physical reserve management work, such as clearing ponds or building paths, helping with visitors and carrying out surveys. An interest in, and some knowledge of, birds is an advantage. Accommodation is free but volunteers pay for their own transport to and from the reserve and provide their own food. Volunteers are required all year round. The minimum age of volunteers is 16 and the minimum period to volunteer is one week (Saturday to Saturday). First-time volunteers have a maximum one-month trial period. Please send a self-addressed label and two first-class stamps to the address below.

Contact: Voluntary Wardens Administrator, The Royal Society for the Protection of Birds, The Lodge, Sandy, Bedfordshire SG19 2DL.

Tel: 01767 680551. Fax: 01767 683262.

Email: volunteers@rspb.org.uk

Website: www.rspb.org.uk/vacancies

RSPB Operation Osprey at Loch Garten   C

Volunteer wardens are required for Operation Osprey at Loch Garten in the ancient Caledonian Forest in Strathspey, Highland. Six volunteers per week are required between 23 March and September 8 2002, to keep a 24-hour watch on the nesting ospreys. Volunteers are expected to maintain the log of osprey activity and guard the nest site and Operation Osprey infrastructure. They will also spend time in the Osprey Centre showing visitors the ospreys, talking to visitors about the RSPB's work at Loch Garten and Abernethy Forest Reserve.

Volunteers work on a shift basis with part of every day free and every third day free. Applicants need to be 18 years or over. It is necessary to take sleeping bag, warm clothing and walking boots.

Contact: RSPB Voluntary Wardening Scheme, The Lodge, Sandy, Bedfordshire SG19 2DL.

Tel: 01767 680551.

Support and Housing Assistance for People with Disabilities (SHAD)   S

SHAD recruits full-time volunteers throughout the year, to act as 'the arms and legs' of severely physically disabled people. Volunteers provide 24-hour cover, working shifts (usually one day on, two days off), and work on a one-to-one basis with disabled tenants, thus enabling them to live independently in their own homes around south-west London. Accommodation, food allowance, pocket money and travel expenses are provided. Volunteering with SHAD provides excellent work experience in a friendly and supportive atmosphere.

About 80 placements are available each year for which no qualifications are required. The minimum length of service is four months and there is no upper limit.

Contact: Volunteer Development Officer, SHAD Wandsworth, 5 Bedford Hill, London SW12 9ET.

Tel: 020 8675 6095.

Email: shadwand@aol.com

Website: www.shad.org.uk

Sustrans   C/W

Each winter, volunteers help organise and participate in work days and weekends across the National Cycle Network, removing encroaching vegetation, clearing culverts, repairing fencing and repainting sculptures. Summer work camps provide an opportunity for volunteers to share their skills and learn new ones whilst helping to construct or improve sections of the Network. These events usually last a couple of weeks; accommodation may be provided in hostels, bunkhouses and tents. Volunteers should be over 16.

Contact: The Manager of Sustrans Volunteer Programme, Sustrans, 35 King Street, Bristol BS1 4DZ.

Tel: 0117 926 8893.

Email: rangers@sustrans.org.uk

Website: www.sustrans.org.uk

Time for God (TFG)   S

TFG places young people (18-25 years) in Christian projects throughout the UK and, once 'matched', ensures the volunteers receive regular support and back-up to enable them to get the most from the experience - this is through regular visits from full-time staff, residential training conferences and frequent contact by phone and letter. Volunteers must either have their own Christian faith, or be actively seeking/exploring Christianity.

Placements involve volunteers becoming part of the staff teams in their placement - whether this is a children's home, a community centre, activity project or a church. The project covers a huge range of client groups including ex-offenders, disabled children, youth groups, drug addicts, the homeless, the elderly and children.

No qualifications are required. TFG will try to make the most of any skills you have. Each placement is unique in terms of what is required from the volunteer and in the benefits the volunteer gains from working there. However, the selection procedure for placements requires completion of a detailed job description and timetable, and TFG staff visits each placement before volunteers are suggested. Volunteers work a maximum of 35-40 hours per week with two days off. Adequate supervision and support and good quality accommodation are provided. Volunteers visit the placement before either side commits itself to the arrangement. Placements are for a minimum of nine and a maximum of twelve months. There will be places for 160 volunteers in 2002/03.

It is advisable to apply in writing to the scheme's office at least two months before the planned start date (September or January).

Contact: Time for God, 2 Chester House, Pages Lane, London N10 1PR.

Tel: 020 8883 1504. Fax: 020 8365 2471.

Email: mail@timeforgod.org

Website: www.timeforgod.org/volunteers

Toc H S

Toc H is a Christian society, originally founded to combat loneliness and hatred and to encourage Christian comradeship among British soldiers after World War I, that now engages in a wide range of social work in the English-speaking world.

Toc H runs short-term residential projects throughout the year, lasting from a weekend up to three weeks. Most of these are in Britain and include working with disabled people, children in need, on playschemes and camps and on conservation projects.

The minimum age is 16, and 18 for some projects. There is no maximum age. EU citizens are given preference. More than 500 volunteers are recruited each year. Further details can be found in the Toc H Volunteer Programme, published annually, at the beginning of March. Early application is advisable.

Contact: Toc H, 1 Forest Close, Wendover, Aylesbury, Buckinghamshire HP22 6BT.

Tel: 01296 623911. Fax: 01296 696137.

Email: info@toch.org.uk

Website: www.toch.org.uk

Waterway Recovery Group C/W

The Waterway Recovery Group is the national coordinating body for voluntary labour on the inland waterways of Britain. It was formed in 1970 to promote and coordinate local trusts and societies involved in restoring abandoned and derelict waterways to a navigable state. Volunteers are needed on summer camps to help with this work. There are many active projects including excavating and laying foundations for a new canal bridge, building walls and parapets, dredging and banking, clearing vegetation, pile-driving, fitting lock gates, bricklaying and demolition work.

Volunteers must be 17 and over; parental consent is required for those under 18. The work is unpaid and sometimes unskilled. Volunteers should be fit, willing to work hard in all weathers and able to live harmoniously in fairly close contact with the other 10-20 volunteers at each camp. Volunteers work for one week or more during June-October, Christmas, February and Easter. Basic accommodation is provided in village halls, or similar, plus three meals a day at a charge of approximately £35 per week. Volunteers should take their own sleeping bag and old clothes, and be prepared to help with domestic chores. Insurance is provided. This work qualifies under the Duke of Edinburgh's Award Scheme. Apply anytime enclosing an SAE. There are, however, limited places.

Contact: The Enquiries Officer, Waterway Recovery Group, PO Box 114, Rickmansworth, Herts WD3 1ZY.

Tel: 01923 711114. Fax: 01923 897000.

Email: enquiries@wrg.org.uk

Website: www.wrg.org.uk

Winged Fellowship Trust S

Winged Fellowship Trust offers care and holidays for people with disabilities and their carers. Volunteers are needed to help socialise with, and aid, the physical care of guests at the four Winged Fellowship Trust holiday centres in the UK. No experience is necessary, as staff are always on hand and training is given. Volunteers' ages vary between 16/17-70; all you need is a commitment to helping the guests and a holiday spirit.

The centres are Sandpipers in Southport, Skylarks in Nottingham, Jubilee Lodge in Essex and Netley Waterside House in Southampton. Winged Fellowship Trust pays travel expenses within the UK and provides board and lodging. Volunteers are required all year round for one to two weeks. There are special weeks such as youth, cricket, horseracing, drama and craft, which are very popular.

Contact: Winged Fellowship Trust, Angel House, 20-32 Pentonville Road, London N1 9XD.

Tel: 020 7833 2594. Fax: 020 7278 0370.

Email: admin@wft.org.uk

Website: www.wft.org.uk

WWOOF UK part of World Wide Opportunities on Organic Farms   C

A countrywide exchange network where bed and board and practical experience are given in return for work on organic farms and smallholdings. Worldwide network. Placements can be anything from three days to several months; individual arrangements are between host and volunteer. Apply anytime for list of contacts (£15 annual subscription). Applicants should be over 18.

Please enclose a SAE.

Contact: WWOOF UK, PO Box 2675, Lewes, Sussex BN7 1RB

Tel/fax: 01273 476286.

Email: hello@wwoof.org

Website: www.wwoof.org

Chapter 8
Using your time to learn and study in the UK

The main reasons for using your gap year to study are:

- to gain vocational skills and qualifications to add to the academic qualifications you have or hope to have

- to continue the habit of study, but in a totally different area from your future higher education course

- to further an interest or hobby which will enrich your quality of life whatever happens in terms of your career

- to sharpen up the brain in the weeks before returning to full-time study, perhaps after a period of travel or voluntary work

- to retrain in order to find a change of job after a career break.

There are often alternatives to traditional full- or part-time college courses, such as by distance learning, in language laboratories or by combining college classes with workplace training.

Vocational courses

There are a number of skills you can learn in a year - or less - which will either enhance your employability at the end of your further or higher education, or which will enable you to find part-time paid work to help finance your studies (a high proportion of students hold part-time jobs during term-time) or full-time work during the vacations. Such skills can always be a second string to your bow if you fail to make it as a brain surgeon, or the degree in drama results in a lot of time 'resting'. Consult the *Directory of Further Education*, published annually by CRAC/Hobsons, in your local college or public reference library. The ECCTIS and TAP databases of courses are available at most careers centres and colleges. The following are just a few ideas for vocational training.

Engineering

The Smallpeice Engineering Careers Foundation Year (ECFY) provides a seven-month course in basic engineering and associated skills. The programme is divided into three parts: three months' academic study at a UK university, one month language tuition at a European language school, and three months' work placement in one of nine countries in Europe (see chapter 11). Applicants pay £30 per week, must be 18 at the start of the programme and must have a deferred university place on an engineering-related degree course.

Contact: The Smallpeice Trust, 74 Upper Holly Walk, Leamington Spa, Warwickshire CV32 4JL.

Tel: 01926 333200. Fax: 01926 333202

Email: gen@smallpeicetrust.org.uk

Website: www.smallpeicetrust.org.uk

Computing

Familiarity with computerised procedures such as spreadsheets, databases, desktop publishing and wordprocessing can often be enough to find you employment without other qualifications, or can be an added bonus if offered alongside a degree or a vocational qualification. Look at job adverts to see what sort of systems are in demand (e.g. Word for Windows, Excel, QuarkXPress, Lotus 1-2-3) and then check your local further education college prospectuses to see what courses they offer. There are also private colleges and training providers which may offer short, intensive courses.

Other office skills

Besides computing, there are courses in secretarial and keyboard skills, administrative procedures, business studies and basic bookkeeping, at further education colleges and in the private sector. As well as a possible source of employment, these can be extremely useful skills for students - taking notes, organising the paperwork, balancing the budget etc!

Complementary and alternative therapies

The major branches of complementary medicine have degree-level qualifications, taking three or more years to complete. But some treatments, such as aromatherapy and reflexology, can easily be learnt in a year.

Contact: Association of Reflexologists, 27 Old Gloucester Street, London WC1N 3XX.

Tel: 0870 567 3320.

Website: www.aor.org.uk

Contact: International Federation of Aromatherapists, 182 Chiswick High Road, London W4 1PP.

Tel 020 8742 2605.

Website: www.int-fed-aromatherapy.co.uk

Contact: Vocational Training Charitable Trust, Customer Service, Unit 11, Brickfield Trading Estate, Brickfield Lane, Chandler's Ford, Hampshire SO53 4DR.

Tel: 023 8027 1733.

The trust can provide a list of colleges running course in aromatherapy, reflexology and holistic therapies. It is also possible to gain counselling qualifications on a one-year full-time course.

Sports instruction

Qualifying to instruct in your chosen sport or for leadership in outdoor pursuits can lead to seasonal or part-time work at recognised sports and outdoor pursuits centres.

Contact: National Coaching Foundation, 114 Cardigan Road, Headingley, Leeds LS6 3BJ.

Tel: 0113 274 4802.

Website: www.ncf.org.uk

Contact: The Outdoor Institute, Eastgate House, Princesshay, Exeter, Devon EX1 1LY.

Tel: 01392 272372.

Website: www.outdoor-learning.org.uk

Flying Fish trains watersports enthusiasts to professional level, in the UK as well as abroad (see chapter 11). Applicants must be 18 by completion of the course. Fees are £1500 plus.

Contact: Flying Fish, 25 Union Road, Cowes, Isle of Wight PO31 7TW.

Tel: 01983 280641. Fax: 01983 281821.

Email: carol.dyer@flyingfishonline.com

Website: www.flyingfishonline.com

Driving

If you don't drive at all, gaining your standard driving licence can be enough for jobs driving small vans - or with further training you can take a test for an LGV licence.

Gaining qualifications in teaching English as a foreign language

This is a very popular way for students and graduates to qualify to earn money whilst seeing the world. There are many opportunities to teach English in the UK, Europe and other areas of the world. A recognised TEFL qualification is often essential, such as the Cambridge Certificate in English Language Teaching to Adults (CELTA) and the Trinity College London Certificate in Teaching English to Speakers of Other Languages (TESOL). These can be gained after an intensive four-week full-time course, but candidates need to be aged 18+, with at least two A levels or equivalent, and a degree is preferred. For information about qualifications and training courses contact:

Contact: Cambridge English Language Teaching, The University of Cambridge Local Examinations Syndicate, Syndicate Buildings, 1 Hills Road, Cambridge CB1 2EU.

Tel: 01223 553789.

Email: efl@ucles.org.uk

Website: www.cambridge-efl.org.uk/teaching

Contact: Trinity College, 89 Albert Embankment, London SE1 7TP.

Tel: 020 7820 6100.

Website: www.trinitycollege.co.uk

Some organisations, such as the following, offer their own in-house TEFL qualification, which may also be recognised by other English language schools.

Inlingua Teacher Training and Recruitment

Offers Trinity Certificate in TESOL, taster courses and Grammar Crammer. For experienced teachers a Certificate in Teaching Business English and Trinity Diploma (distance learning). Free recruitment service to all successful candidates.

Contact: Inlingua Teacher Training and Recruitment, Rodney Lodge, Rodney Road, Cheltenham GL50 1HX.

Tel: 01242 253171. Fax: 01242 253181

Email: training@inlingua-cheltenham.co.uk

Website: www.inlingua-cheltenham.co.uk

Languages Training and Development

LT and D is a provider of TESOL and the London Chamber of Commerce and Industry Foundation Certificate for Teachers of Business English. Based in Witney and Barcelona. Can combine training with a work placement on a distance basis. They offer programmes lasting from four weeks to a year.

Contact: Languages Training and Development, 116 Corn Street, Witney, Oxford OX28 6BU.

Tel: 01993 894710. Fax: 01993 706066.

Email: info@ltdoxford.com

Website: www.ltdoxford.com

i-to-i

Intensive 20-hour weekend TEFL courses are offered at venues nationwide.

Contact: i-to-i, 9 Blenheim Terrace, Leeds LS2 9HZ.

Tel: 0870 333 2332.

Website: www.i-to-i.com

If in doubt, check with the British Council (address below) or the Association of Recognised English Language Services, 56 Buckingham Gate, London SW1E 6AG (telephone: 020 7802 9200). www.arels.org.uk

How to become a Teacher of English is a leaflet available from the British Council Information Centre, Bridgewater House, 58 Whitworth Street, Manchester M1 6BB. Tel: 0161 957 7384. Website: www.britishcouncil.org

TEFL courses are often advertised in the education section of *The Guardian* on Tuesdays and in the *Times Educational Supplement* on Fridays. See chapters 6 and 9 for employment opportunities.

Academic study and learning for pleasure

There is a lot of overlap with these two types of study, as academic subjects can be decidedly pleasurable. The obvious source of information on one-year full- or part-time academic courses is your local further education college, or see the *Directory of Further Education* mentioned under the heading of vocational courses.

If you are looking for short courses, there are numerous options. Most universities and colleges of higher education offer a wide assortment of subjects at summer schools, usually lasting one or two weeks. Many of these are featured in *The Guardian* weekend editions in early summer. The British Trust for Conservation Volunteers and the Field Studies Council offer short residential courses in various biological and environmental topics, ranging from hedgelaying to botanical illustration. Many of the above courses are listed in *Time to Learn* published by City and Guilds London Institute (see bibliography in Part 5 for details).

Adult Residential Colleges Association (ARCA)

Comprises 31 colleges throughout England and Wales which offer short residential courses - some run by local authorities, some by charitable trusts and some private. An enormous range of subjects is offered at day, weekend or one-week courses.

Contact: Secretary, ARCA, PO Box 31, Washbrook, Ipswich, Suffolk IP8 3HF.

Email: john@newco.freeserve.co.uk

Website: www.aredu.org.uk

Stratford-upon-Avon College - Year Out Drama

An exciting, challenging, intensive, practical drama course specific to gap-year students, with the option to gain theatre studies A level. Students benefit from working with theatre experts in professionally-equipped performance spaces, on varying disciplines including acting techniques, voice, movement, directing, text study and performance. Students perform annually at the Edinburgh Fringe Festival.

The course is designed for students intending to enter HE, but not exclusively those aiming for a career in theatre. The publicity booklet includes destinations of former students.

The course runs from September to July, split into three terms, and costs £3900 for the year, which includes all production costs, travel and tickets for frequent theatre trips. Accommodation costs are extra, in accommodation blocks, with landladies or in shared houses.

Students are given help with auditions and UCAS applications. The company has strong support from The Royal Shakespeare Company and other working professionals.

Contact: Deborah Moody, Stratford-upon-Avon College, Alcester Road, Stratford-upon-Avon CV37 9QR.

Tel: 01789 266245. Fax: 01789 267524.

Email: college@strat-avon.ac.uk

Website: www.strat-avon.ac.uk

Learning another language

Learning a new language, or brushing up on one you learned at school, is particularly useful if you intend to travel as part of your gap year or in the future. Again, the obvious place to do this is your local further education college, but there are also some specialist private institutions which may offer more intensive courses with more individual attention, such as the following.

Alliance Française

Alliance Française runs French courses in London, France and worldwide.

Contact: Alliance Française, 1 Dorset Square, London NW1 6PU.

Tel: 020 7723 6439.

Email: info@alliancefrancaise.org.uk

Website: www.alliancefrancaise.org.uk

Anglo World Education (UK) Limited

Runs courses in Bournemouth, Cambridge, London, Oxford and Edinburgh.

Contact: Aspects International Language Academies, Heliting House, Richmond Hill, Bournemouth, Dorset BH2 6HT.

Tel: 01202 638100.

Email: daniele.schembri@aspectworld.com

Website: www.aspectworld.com

Institut Français

The Institut Français runs French courses in London.

Contact: Institut Français, 14 Cromwell Place, South Kensington, London SW7 2JR.

Tel: 020 7581 2701.

Email: eric.chevreul@ambafrance.org.uk

Website: www.institut.ambafrance.org.uk

International House

International House runs language courses in London and at affiliated schools abroad.

Contact: International House, 106 Piccadilly, London W1J 7NL.

Tel: 020 7518 6999. Fax: 020 7518 6998.

Email: info@ihlondon.co.uk

Website: www.ihlondon.com

Retraining for a new career

Most of the courses we have mentioned so far in this chapter have been at further education level. Many people who already have a degree feel that, for whatever reason, they would like a change, and decide to take a postgraduate course in something completely different, to change their career direction.

Profile **Jill Hind**

Training for archaeology

'I had always wanted to teach and, armed with a chemistry degree, I worked my way up the career ladder of secondary education. After posts as Head of Year and Head of Department I took up a management position as well as being in charge of chemistry. By then I was working every evening and weekend without feeling I was on top of it. More importantly, after 23 years I had stopped enjoying teaching and if you don't enjoy it, you don't do it well.

It was time to change. Options included archaeology, a longstanding interest in which I had been taking courses for seven years. If I wanted another career I needed to be taken seriously by potential employers; so, after debating whether we could afford my taking a year off, I signed up for the Postgraduate Diploma in Professional Archaeology at Oxford University. This course provides four work placements, backed up by short courses and written assignments, based on how the profession works. I was fortunate to have the support of my partner, as finance was the biggest problem for fellow students.

Three placements were a local authority, a commercial organisation, and a national body while one was specific to my particular qualifications and interests. While the whole year was fun, stimulating and varied, the highlight was definitely a project on the chemical analysis of pottery.

Towards the end of the course I began applying for jobs. I wrote a letter of inquiry to the Oxford Archaeological Unit (my third placement) and was offered a short-term contract for one project. Then other projects arose leading to promotion and a permanent contract. The work is varied, mainly preparing reports on the archaeological potential of development sites before work begins.

I decided to convert my diploma into a Master of Studies in my spare time. After graduation I was invited to become a part-time tutor for adult education and am now preparing my first course. Full circle!

The benefits from my career change include restoration of self-confidence, a good night's sleep and time and energy to enjoy a social life. I have also gained academic and intellectual stimulation.

I do not regret teaching and enjoyed most of my service, but giving up was not an easy decision. One of the biggest worries was whether I would be able to break into another profession in my 40s, but this proved unfounded.'

3

Taking time
out abroad

Chapter 9
Paid employment abroad

There are a variety of opportunities open to those of you who want to spend time out undertaking paid employment in a different country. These range from au pairing in Italy to working on farms in the Australian outback! The rates of pay you can expect will vary considerably; some opportunities described within this chapter, such as au pair work, offer only a basic level of pay - in effect pocket money - as accommodation and other expenses are all paid for. Other opportunities offer higher rates of remuneration. You will need to balance up the experience you will gain against the money you hope to earn!

Information about opportunities offered by organisations listed in this chapter have been grouped as follows:

- organised work placement/working holiday programmes
- working as an au pair or nanny
- teaching English as a foreign language
- tourism-related work (including work on children's summer camps)
- career-related work placements during/after your higher education course.

For some opportunities, you will need a good grasp of the language of your destination country. For others, basic language skills can suffice. There are also plenty of opportunities in the USA and other English speaking countries, where language is not (generally!) a barrier.

Work permits

Work permits are not required to work in other EU countries. You must, however, check with the relevant embassy whether a residence permit is required.

Those who are intending to work outside of the EU will need to apply for a work permit; contact the relevant embassy for information (addresses in Part 5). If you are using the services of an organisation to arrange your placement, the organisation will obtain the necessary visas/permits for you. Governments in many countries support those organisations running approved exchanges and short-term working programmes, so the organisations are able to obtain the necessary documentation smoothly. If you intend to fix up your own job independently, you will need to apply for your own work permit. This may be difficult to acquire, as many countries restrict the numbers entering their country for work purposes. Applicants with skills for which there is a demand may find it easier to get a work permit. Sometimes you can get caught in the 'you can't get a work permit unless you have a job' dilemma. Embassies can provide you with all the necessary information about working regulations etc.

Australia and New Zealand offer **working holiday visas** to young people wishing to undertake short-term casual work as part of a holiday. A number of the organisations listed later in this chapter arrange working holidays to these countries, under the working visa schemes.

Applicants for an Australian working holiday visa must be aged between 18-30. Visas last for twelve months. Holders can undertake casual work in Australia, with each job lasting no more than three months. You have to show that you have sufficient funds for the fare to your intended destination on leaving Australia, and enough money for your personal support while in Australia. For more information, contact the Australian High Commission (address in Part 5) or visit their website: www.australia.org.uk

The New Zealand High Commission operates a working holiday scheme whereby UK citizens aged 18-30 can visit New Zealand for up to 12 months, and undertake temporary casual work. Numbers are limited; a yearly quota system applies. Applicants need the equivalent of NZ$4,200 to finance their trip. For more details contact the New Zealand High Commission Immigration line on 090 69 100 100. See also their website: www.immigration.govt.nz

Insurance

Whichever country you are visiting, it is important to arrange adequate insurance cover for accidents, sickness and loss of possessions.

If you are travelling under the auspices of one of the organisations running work placement programmes, insurance may be included as part of the package, but this is not always the case. If you are intending to work in a European Union country, UK residents are entitled to reciprocal medical treatment in other EU countries i.e. you get treatment on the same terms as a citizen of that country. To be entitled to this, you need a certificate E111, available through post offices, before you go. It is sensible to consider taking out private health insurance beyond this, however.

There are many companies offering insurance packages, and some specialise in insurance and other services for students. Chapter 12 provides further information.

Finding opportunities

Many of the jobs advertised in the national press and other journals are for applicants with particular skills, experience and qualifications, and may be opportunities of a longer-term nature than you have in mind. There are, however, a number of programmes offering shorter-term employment opportunities, including working holidays and short-term working placements in the USA, Canada and various other countries.

Overseas Jobs Express, issued twice monthly, carries a wide range of job advertisements, and includes features on topics like working on cruise ships, at skiing resorts etc. For subscription enquiries tel: 01273 699611. Subscription costs: £39 for three months, £70 for six months. Website: www.overseasjobsexpress.co.uk

Opportunities Abroad is a bulletin publishing vacancies in development work overseas. For subscription details contact World Service Enquiry, Room 233, Bon Marché Centre, 241-251 Ferndale Road, London SW9 8BJ. Tel: 020 7346 5950. The bulletin is also available on their website: www.wse.org.uk

How to Books and Vacation Work are publishers of a number of books on finding work abroad, such as Vacation Work's publications *Summer Jobs Abroad*, *Summer Jobs USA* and *Work Your Way Around the World*. Full details of useful publications are given in Part 5 of this book.

EURES offers access to vacancies in Europe (see below).

Opportunities in the European Union

Through the continuing integration of Europe, many companies with bases in the UK have developed partnerships with companies in other parts of Europe, or have branches in other EU member states. When recruiting, employers usually look for applicants with relevant qualifications and experience, and good communication skills in the language of the country concerned.

EURES (European Employment Services) is a system of exchanging vacancies between the 15 countries of the European Union. In the UK, it is possible to access a database of European vacancies via Jobcentres, and there are also several Euro-advisers working at bases throughout the UK. They are regularly in touch with their counterparts abroad, and can give people advice about working and living in other European countries. They can also put you in touch with the Employment Service in the country you want to go to. Contact your local Jobcentre or The Overseas Placing Unit, Level 1, Rockingham House, 123 West Street, Sheffield S1 4ER. Tel: 0114 259 6000. The OPU is the UK co-ordinator of the EURES network and produces a series of fact sheets on working in all the European Union countries.

If you have been registered as a job seeker in the UK for at least four weeks, and are in receipt of contributory-based Jobseeker's Allowance, you may continue to receive UK unemployment benefit for up to three months, while seeking work in the EU.

Making your own contacts

If you are looking independently for short-term work abroad, you could contact potential employers directly - particularly those who may offer seasonal work, such as hotel and other tourist-related opportunities. If you are looking for a particular kind of job, one starting point may be to research relevant companies that have bases in other countries, and see if they can offer you any opportunities.

Don't feel shy of making use of any personal contacts who may be able to introduce you to a potential employer abroad. If your local town/city is involved in a twinning arrangement with towns in Europe or further afield where you would consider working, you may be able to find some contacts to get you started. Make sure that you have the necessary language skills, however, for any position you are aiming for - while basic local language skills may be all that is necessary for working as a waitress in a café, working as a hotel receptionist will demand a higher level of communication skills.

Instead of finding your own job opportunities, applying for visas etc, you could let one of the organisations described below do the 'leg work' for you.

Organisations offering work placements/ working holiday programmes

You may find the prospect of travelling under the auspices of a reputable organisation less daunting than sorting out your arrangements independently. Such organisations/agencies have bases in the UK and can organise travel arrangements, work permits, visas, insurance, provide orientation sessions and back-up, and may organise your accommodation for the first night or two. They provide you with listings and information about job vacancies - all for a fee, of course! When researching such organisations, look carefully at the services they offer and fees they charge. Some of the organisations can offer access to a wide range of job opportunities, in a number of countries. A further advantage of using such organisations is that they can provide a way of getting to know other people who are undertaking similar placements in the same area. The size of your pay packet will vary according to the work you are undertaking.

The remainder of this section lists organisations who offer work placement abroad and working holiday programmes. Some organisations provide work placements specifically for students wishing to gain some career-related work experience during their higher education course (or immediately after), in order to gain experience in their chosen field. Details of such organisations are given later in this chapter, under the section 'Undertaking a career-related work placement during (or shortly after) your higher education course'.

AgriVenture

AgriVenture is run by the International Agricultural Exchange Association and arranges programmes for young agriculturalists/ horticulturalists to experience work and culture in USA, Canada, New Zealand or Japan. You must be a British citizen aged between 18 and 30, have a full driving licence, and good practical experience.

Trips to USA, Canada, Australia and Japan depart in the Spring and trips to Australia and New Zealand leave in the Autumn. There are several 'around the world trips' which also leave in the autumn. Most programmes last between six months and a year.

Selection procedures and orientation consists of local interviews, pre-departure meetings and seminars on arrival in your chosen country. The organisers aim to find you a host who will best suit your experience, wishes and interests and provide full back up.

Participants pay from £1800, which includes airline tickets, transfers in hosting country, visas, insurance, seminars and full back-up. A realistic wage is paid with board and lodging being provided by the host family. Time off for unpaid holidays is also included.

Contact: AgriVenture (IAEA), YFC Centre, National Agricultural Centre, Stoneleigh Park, Kenilworth, Warwickshire CV8 2LG.

Freephone: 0800 783 2186

Email: uk@agriventure.com

Website: www.agriventure.com

Profile   James Gatward
'No worries' – to New Zealand with AgriVenture

'I always imagined that I would pass my A levels and then progress to a good university, which would lead me to the perfect career. How wrong I was! It turned out that months of revision would crumble away in the exam hall leaving me struggling to remember how to describe the importance of a phospholipid in the human body. The experience left me physically and mentally strained as well as completely confused about, well, everything!

The solution to my problems came in the form of a father and son talk where my Dad turned to me and suggested that I took a year out. Not that he wanted to get rid of me – then, maybe he did. My brother previously spent nine months in Australia working on a sheep farm organised through AgriVenture and it was his praise of the experience that got me hooked on the idea.

At an information day I found out about all the options and, before I knew it, I was on an aeroplane bound for the bottom of the world – New Zealand. AgriVenture arranged my placement on a dairy farm (North Island), booked my flights, arranged insurance and sorted out a stopover in Singapore, as well as many other things.

Fitting into the way of life in New Zealand was easy with everyone making me feel welcome. It wasn't long before I realised that the people live at a different pace of life than the rest of the world – more like a stroll in the park than a mad rush for the bus.

Not every waking moment was fun, though perhaps the hardest part was catching the flight back 'home'. There were times when things would get a bit tense – when the cows tried to recreate the Great Escape or I remodelled the tractor by wrapping it around an electric fence – my host family seemed to understand and just shrugged it off.

Much of my time off I spent driving around in my 1987 Honda, touring the country and visiting friends on other farms. I made sure I saw as much of New Zealand as I could. This included travelling to *the South Island with my visiting brother for a two-week holiday. I won't go into details but I'm sure you can picture the sort of things two brothers would get up to in a beautiful country with an exchange rate of $3 to £1... All I will say is that jumping out of an aeroplane at 12,000 ft and free-falling for 45 seconds is the best excuse I can think of for having a strong drink in a 5* hotel. Marvellous!*

Having a year out was, without doubt, the best thing I could have done. I changed a lot in my time away. I built self-confidence, became independent, developed a better knowledge of farming and machinery, as well as coming back with a great suntan. The year also gave me time to think – I decided to go into estate management and was accepted at agricultural college.

With my year out complete and my university days just beginning, I can honestly say that I've got 'no worries', even though I still don't know how to describe the importance of a phospholipid...'

The Army Gap Year Commissions Scheme

Army Gap Year Commissions are offered to young people aged 18 - 20 years, who have already gained a university place. Successful applicants often serve abroad. For full details, see their entry in chapter 6.

ATD Fourth World

ATD works with the poorest and most disadvantaged in society, and offers long-term opportunities paying a basic salary and NI contributions. For further details, see their entry in chapter 10.

BUNAC - British Universities North America Club

BUNAC offers work/travel programmes in America, Australia, Canada, Ghana, New Zealand, South Africa and Costa Rica. Under these programmes BUNAC organises the visa and travel arrangements, provides back-up support, and information and advice about employment opportunities. Their programmes offering employment on children's summer camps in the USA are described in the section later in this chapter covering tourism-related work.

Work American and KAMP

Work America Programme (WAP) and Kitchen and Maintenance Programme (KAMP) offer students studying full-time at HND or degree level (or, for the KAMP programme, an appropriate level catering course) the chance to work in a variety of jobs during the summer months (June-September). Students in their gap year, who are at least 18, and who have an unconditional higher education place for the following autumn, can also apply. WAP entitles you to take any job in the USA, and KAMP entitles you to do a variety of non-counselling jobs on summer camps. The registration fee for the WAP programme is £89. Participants pay for their own flight and insurance. It costs £62 to register for the KAMP programme and participants also pay for their own insurance.

Work Australia

Work Australia offers young people aged 18-30 (inclusive) the chance to live and work in Australia for up to one year. The programme features a round-trip flight, working holiday visa, Bangkok stopover (if flying from London), Hawaii stopover (if flying from Los Angeles), ongoing support and assistance, mail forwarding, orientations and two nights' accommodation in Sydney. Applicants must be citizens of the UK, Canada, the Republic of Ireland or the Netherlands. In 2001, fees for this programme, for participants flying from the UK, ranged from £1537 to £1850.

Work Canada

This scheme provides a general work permit valid for a twelve-month period which authorises the student to take up any job anywhere in Canada. To be eligible for this programme, applicants must be aged 18-29 and currently in higher education in the UK. Students in their gap year, and who are at least 18, can apply if they have an unconditional place in university-level education for the following autumn. The fee for this programme is £95. In addition, it is necessary to pay for your own flight and insurance cover.

Contact: BUNAC, 16 Bowling Green Lane, London EC1R 0QH.
Tel: 020 7251 3472. Fax: 020 7251 0215.
Website: www.bunac.org.uk

Changing Worlds

Changing Worlds offer paid placements in a number of countries. Placements include working in the Canadian ski resorts of Banff or Whistler, and opportunities in tourism and farm work in Australia and New Zealand. Placements can last three or six months. Applicants with initiative, determination, adaptability and social skills are sought. Relevant experience and qualifications are welcome, but not essential. Participants' ages range from 18-35 years. Changing Worlds also offers unpaid voluntary placements.

Prices start from £1695, according to the placement. This includes flights, orientation on arrival in-country, accommodation, and pre-departure briefing. Departure dates are September, January and March. Apply as early as you can.

Contact: *Changing Worlds, 11 Doctors Lane, Chaldon, Surrey CR3 5AE.*
Tel: 01883 340960. Fax: 01883 330783.
Email: careers@changingworlds.co.uk
Website: www.changingworlds.co.uk

Council on International Educational Exchange (Council Exchanges)

Council Exchanges, a registered UK charitable trust, offers work abroad programmes to the USA, Canada, Australia, New Zealand, China, Thailand, and Japan, as well as language study programmes (see chapter 11). Council Exchanges has over 400 staff based in 12 countries, with a network of partner organisations in a further 61 countries. In the year 2000, Council Exchanges dealt with over 50,000 participants.

Work & Travel Australia and Work & Travel New Zealand

The Work & Travel Australia programme allows 18-30 year-olds to travel in Australia for up to twelve months, taking casual work along the way. Participants on the programme can take jobs for up to three months at a time, and can work in any part of Australia. Work & Travel New Zealand offers a similar experience in New Zealand. Participants also have the option of combining the two programmes.

Work & Travel USA

Work & Travel USA is a summer work programme which allows participants to take almost any job, anywhere in the USA, anytime between June and October. Gap year students with an unconditional offer at a UK college/university are eligible, as are full-time students at HND level and recent graduates. Participants have the flexibility to arrange a job before they go or upon arrival and are supplied with pre-departure and post-arrival support in the US. Council Exchanges acts as legal sponsor to get the necessary visa for working in the USA.

See also their entries later in this chapter, under headings 'Teaching English as a foreign language' and 'Undertaking a career-related work placement during your higher education course'.

Contact: *Council Exchanges, 52 Poland Street, London W1V 4JQ.*
Tel: 020 7478 2020. Fax: 020 7478 7322.
Email: infoUK@councilexchanges.org.uk
Website: www.councilexchanges.org.uk

EIL – Work and Travel USA

EIL is a charity specialising in educational travel, and offers a variety of gap-year opportunities (described in chapters 10 and 11). Under their Work and Travel USA programme, full-time students can work legally in the USA, between June and October. Minimum eight weeks work, followed by one month of travelling. Approximate cost is £400 plus international travel and insurance.

Contact: EIL, 287 Worcester Road, Malvern, Worcs, WR14 1AB.

Tel: 01684 562577. Fax: 01684 562212.

Email: info@eiluk.org

Website: www.eiluk.org

i-to-i

Working holidays in the Australian Outback. Applicants should be 18 plus.

Contact: i-to-i, 9 Blenheim Terrace, Leeds LS2 9HZ.

Tel: 0870 333 2332. Fax: 0113 274 6923.

Email: travel@i-to-i.com

Website: www.i-to-i.com

International Health Exchange

The Exchange only recruits qualified health workers with at least two years' post-qualification experience on behalf of international relief and development agencies.

Contact: International Health Exchange, 134 Lower Marsh, London SE1 7AE.

Tel: 020 7620 3333. Fax: 020 7620 2277.

Email: info@ihe.org.uk

Website: www.ihe.org.uk

Skillshare International

Skillshare International offers opportunities for skilled, qualified and experienced people to undertake placements from six months to two years in Africa and Asia. Skillshare is included in this listing as participants receive an allowance sufficient to maintain 'a reasonable standard of living' whilst they are on placement. For more details, see their entry in chapter 10.

VisitOZ

This organisation provides opportunities for young people to work in Australia on the land or in rural hospitality, for up to three months with any one employer.

Contact: VisitOZ, 4C Queens Gate Place, London SW7 5NT.

Tel: 020 7581 8627.

Website: visitoz.org

Voluntary Service Overseas (VSO)

VSO is mentioned in this chapter as the volunteers do receive some remuneration while in post. VSO recruits volunteers who work in the fields of education, natural resources, the health services, technical trades and engineering, business and social work. Work takes place in over 70 developing countries. VSO pays fares and various grants, health insurance and NI contributions. The overseas employer provides accommodation and a salary based on local rates.

For more details, see their entry in chapter 10.

Work Experience USA and Work Experience Down Under

Work Experience USA

An opportunity for full-time students aged 19 - 28 to gain work experience tailored to their individual needs in the USA. For a fee of £725, applicants receive return fare, insurance, visa, two days' orientation in New York, and a job offer for from ten weeks up to four months between June and September, paying an average wage of $4.50 to $10 per hour. Example jobs include working on a ranch in Colorado, at the Grand Canyon National Park or at a resort in New York. Apply as early as possible between September and April.

Work Experience Down Under

Work Experience Down Under is a new programme. It is for those aged 18-30, and allows you to work and travel in Australia or New Zealand for up to 12 months.

Contact: Work Experience USA & Down Under, Green Dragon House, 64-70 High Street, Croydon, Surrey CRO 9XN.

Tel: 020 8688 9051. Fax: 020 8681 8168.

Email: inquiry@ccusaweusa.co.uk

Website: www.workexperienceusa.com

Zentralstelle für Arbeitsvermittlung (ZAV)

ZAV can find and organise two- to three-month summer posts for students aged 18-30. Applicants should have studied German for at least four years, and be able to provide proof of university enrolment with dates of beginning and end of summer term holidays.

Contact: Zentralstelle für Arbeitsvermittlung, Dept.21.22, Villemomblerstrasse 76, 53123 Bonn, Germany.

Tel: 00 49 228 713 1330.

Email: bonn-zav.info-auslaendische-studenten@arbeitsamt.de

Working as an au pair or nanny

Perhaps one of the easiest jobs to find abroad is that of an au pair or nanny. There are a number of agencies, many of which are based in the UK, that recruit nannies and au pairs for countries within Europe and further afield, for positions ranging from one month to a year. Applicants should be 18; some agencies set an upper age of 26-30. Formal childcare qualifications are not essential, although childcare experience such as babysitting is required. The more childcare experience you have, the easier you will find the work. Most of all, to be a successful au pair you have to be flexible and willing to adapt to a different way of life.

Some knowledge of the language of the country is sometimes necessary, and often au pairs/nannies are given time off to attend language classes, which may be paid for. Full board and lodging are provided and the average pocket money per week is around £40, but it is possible to earn more than this.

Hours of work expected vary, but au pairs/nannies usually work about 30 or more hours a week over six days. They may have to do some light housework in addition to looking after the children, and may be asked to babysit in the evening. Some agencies require references and applicants need to be physically fit. A full driving licence will be needed for some positions.

A number of agencies specialise in sending au pairs to USA, with the support of the US government. The conditions are generally the same for all. Applicants should usually be aged 18-26, have childcare experience (e.g. babysitting) or a childcare qualification (e.g. CACHE Diploma/NNEB, BTEC) and a full driving licence. Applicants may be asked to provide a returnable good faith deposit to ensure their commitment. Au pairs work for twelve months looking after children, and often also undertake light housework. Au pairs are given a year's visa and receive an allowance. Paid for expenses can include a return flight, medical insurance, funding towards a course, board and lodging in the family home, two weeks' paid holiday and the support of a local counsellor during the stay. Au pairs usually attend an orientation session on arrival in America, and get to know other au pairs in their area.

Below, you will find the details of agencies that recruit nannies and au pairs. It is worth applying to several different agencies, so that you have a choice of family and area in the country of your choice. Investigate how much support the agencies offer. If you have problems with your family, is there a local representative to help you? If you hope to have contact with other au pairs/nannies during your stay, will there be others in the area? Are you sure you understand what duties will be expected of you? Find out as much as you can before you make a commitment.

Accueil Familial des Jeunes Etrangers

Accueil Familial des Jeunes Etrangers arranges for au pairs aged 18-27 to stay with French families all over France. Applicants must be able to speak some French. Summer placements are arranged from one to three months; longer stays, until the end of the school year in July, start 1-15 September and 1-15 January. The agency also provides accommodation through its paying guest service. It is preferable that applications should be made two months before the proposed starting date of work, although it is possible for the agency to find a family in less time, but at least two weeks is required.

Contact: Accueil Familial des Jeunes Etrangers, 23 rue du Cherche-Midi, 75006 Paris, France.

Tel: 00 33 1 4222 5034. Fax: 00 33 1 4544 6048.

Email: accueil@afje-paris.org

Au Pair in America

Run by the American Institute for Foreign Study, Au Pair in America places au pairs with American families for 12 months. Flights, pocket money of around $248 per week for up to 45 hours/week childcare, and an allowance towards an educational course are provided. Qualified and experienced childcarers may enter the Au Pair Extraordinaire programme, receiving an enhanced pocket money allowance ($317/week). Their new 'EduCare' programme offers child support for families with older children.

Contact: Au Pair in America, 37 Queen's Gate, London SW7 5HR.

Tel: 020 7581 7300.

Website: www.afis.com

Profile **Samantha Child**

To the USA with Au Pair in America

'I had just finished my degree and felt pretty disillusioned with the job market. I needed a complete change especially after a stressful final year at university. I decided to spend a year in the States with 'Au Pair in America'. The brochure explained the programme in detail and they offered the support of a Community Counsellor.

The application process was very detailed. Along with the application form, I had to write a 'Dear host family' letter introducing myself and also send photographs with references, educational certificates, driving licence and criminal record check.

At the interview we chatted about my expectations of life with an American family and providing childcare. My references were telephone checked and my doctor completed a medical report. I was accepted onto the programme and my application form was circulated to families I might be compatible with.

I didn't feel comfortable with the first family who called. However, with the second family everything just clicked into place. They told me about their family and where they lived. They explained about my daily routine and what they expected of me. We also had similar interests and expectations, so I accepted their offer.

My first four days in America were spent near New York on orientation, with au pairs from other countries. We learnt about the American culture, first aid, personal and child safety. It definitely prepared me for the year ahead.

I then flew to Raleigh, North Carolina to my host family. The first three days was a big adjustment period for us all, learning about each other. During the first month I established my routine with the girls, aged five years and thirteen months, and made friends with the other au pairs in my 'cluster' group. My Community Counsellor kept in regular contact. Throughout the year I got to travel and see different parts of the States; one of my favourite places was Washington D.C.

Au pairing for 45 hours a week is hard work - some days it's difficult to find exciting ways to occupy a five-year-old while coping with a toddler! However, it is very rewarding sharing in the development of a child's life and watching them grow.

I am back now, living and working in England. I am still in close contact with my family and we speak regularly on the phone. I had a fantastic year in America, one I will never forget.'

Au Pair International

Au Pair International places au pairs in Italy in the summer (June-September) or longer term (for periods of six, nine or twelve months from September). The work is mostly childminding, with some housework. Pocket money is approximately £40 per week, plus full board and lodging. Au pairs work approximately six hours per day, with one complete day and two or three evenings free per week. Applicants should be aged 18-30; babysitting experience is an advantage.

Contact: Au Pair International sas, via S Stefano 32, 40125 Bologna, Italy.

Tel: 00 39 051 267575/238320. Fax: 00 39 051 236594.
Email: info@au-pair-international.com
Website: www.au-pair-international.com

Childcare International Ltd

Childcare America

Visa-supported, one-year stays in the USA are arranged for applicants aged 18-26. Childcare experience is required; drivers and non-smokers are preferred. Applicants can choose their host family and they will have the opportunity to attend a part-time college course. Support is available from a local counsellor. Return air fare and medical insurance is paid, plus two weeks' vacation. Applicants can start at any time and can earn $140-$165 per week, depending on qualifications.

Childcare Canada

Provides live-in family placements in Canada for those with a nanny/teaching/nursing qualification. The minimum stay is one year and applicants must be over 18. Support and assistance are given throughout the stay.

Contact: Childcare International Ltd, Trafalgar House, Grenville Place, London NW7 3SA.

Tel: 020 8959 3611 or 020 8906 3116. Fax: 020 8906 3461.

Email: office@childint.co.uk

Website: www.childint.co.uk

Club de Relaciones Culturales Internacionales (RCI)

Club de RCI is a cultural, educational and language association which has extensive international programmes for students and adults from Spain and other countries. People from the UK may be interested in their au pair in Spain programme. This programme places foreign students in families in Spain. Au pairs are asked to help with the children for five hours a day, with languages, babysitting and light housework. In return, they live as a member of the family, with board and lodging provided, and receive a weekly allowance. Club de RCI offers au pairs in Spain beginners, intermediate and advanced level classes in Spanish. It also organises au pair programmes, study abroad programmes for Spanish students, and a language assistant programme, where you live with a family and assist and tutor the family in English for 15 hrs/week.

Contact: Club de Relaciones Culturales Internacionales, Departmento Socio-Cultural, Ferraz, 82, 28008 Madrid, Spain.

Tel: 00 34 1 541 71 03.

Inter-Séjours

Inter-Séjours places au pairs in Austria, Australia, the Balearic Islands, Canada, Denmark, France, Germany, Great Britain, Ireland, Italy, The Netherlands, New Zealand, Spain, Sweden and USA. Duties include light housework and looking after children, from 15 to 30 hours per week. Work is for two to 24 months at any time throughout the year. Full board accommodation, individual room, pocket money and free time to attend classes and time off are all included. Applicants should be aged 18-30 and have some knowledge of the language of the country they wish to visit. Pocket money is around £150 per month in France and Germany. Paying guests can also stay with families in France (many families within the Loire valley), Germany, Italy and Spain and in the USA. Two or three hours of lessons per day plus sporting activities and excursions can be arranged if required.

Contact: Inter-Séjours, 179 rue de Courcelles, 75017 Paris, France.

Tel: 00 33 1 4763 0681. Fax: 00 33 1 4054 8941.

Email: marie.inter-sejours@libertysurf.fr

Website: www.multimania.com/intersejours/index.html

Séjours Internationaux Linguistiques et Culturels

This organisation places au pairs with families in France for a minimum of eight weeks in the summer, or for six months or more (preferably a school year) starting in September.

Contact: SILC, c/o Christiane Burt, Euro-Pair Agency, 28 Derwent Avenue, Pinner, Middlesex HA5 4QJ.

Tel: 020 8421 2100. Fax: 020 8428 6416.

Email: europair@btinternet.com

Website: www.euro-pair.co.uk

Or

Contact: Séjours Internationaux, 32 Rempart de l'Est,

16022 Angouleme, Cedex, France.

Tel: 00 33 5 4597 4110.

Solihull Au Pair and Nanny Agency and Edgeware Au Pair Agency

Arranges one year au pair placements in the USA with the Au Pair Care Cultural Exchange Programme, and six months to one year placements in several European countries - mainly France, Spain, Italy and Germany. For the USA, applicants must be 18-26 years, with a driving licence and childcare experience. A $500 deposit is required and $100 for insurance. Au pairs are paid $138 per week. Au pairs for European countries must be aged 18-27, with childcare experience, and some practical knowledge of the European language. Payment in Europe is £40-£60 a week.

Contact: Solihull Au Pair and Nanny Agency/Edgeware Au Pair Agency, 1565 Stratford Road, Hall Green, Birmingham B28 9JA.

Tel: 0121 733 6444. Fax: 0121 733 6555.

Email: lorraine@au-pairs4u.com

Website: www.100saupairs.co.uk

WorldNetUK

Childcare in the USA – there are two programmes. Those with childcare qualifications, such as the CACHE Diploma in Childcare and Education (formerly NNEB), BTEC National Diploma in Nursery Nursing, or NVQ level 3 may apply for the 'au pair extraordinaire' programme. Unqualified applicants with childcare/babysitting experience can apply for the regular au pair programme. Applicants for both programmes must be between 18-26, and hold a full driving licence, and are provided with free return flights, two weeks' paid holiday, an education allowance and other benefits.

Ski/summer resort nannies – with all major travel companies in various European destinations. Applicants must be qualified/experienced in childcare to work either in activity clubs, crèches or with individual families. No age limits. Applicants must be available for either the full summer or ski season (although some shorter-term placements are sometimes available).

Contact: WorldNetUK, Emberton House, 26 Shakespeare Road, Bedford MK40 2ED.

Tel: 07002 287247 for a brochure. Fax: 01234 351070.

Email: info@worldnetuk.com

Website: www.worldnetuk.com

Teaching English as a foreign language (TEFL)

There are many opportunities to teach English abroad. Employment is available with language schools, international agencies, foreign companies and governments. Positions occur in a wide range of countries. Employment is usually on the basis of short-term contracts, making TEFL a popular option for those who wish to take a temporary break.

A recognised TEFL qualification, such as the Cambridge Certificate or Diploma, or the Trinity College London Certificate or Diploma, is usually a requirement, and applicants may also need to be graduates.

Further information about TEFL qualifications and how to obtain them is given in chapter 8.

People without TEFL qualifications and experience can find opportunities through some of the voluntary work opportunities described in chapter 10, including those offered by Teaching Abroad and i-to-i.

Knowledge of a foreign language is not always necessary to teach English abroad.

Finding opportunities

- The *EL Gazette*, published every month, includes a recruitment section. Subscription for the Gazette, comprising articles and information about TEFL, is £32/year or £20/six months. Subscriptions are handled by T G Scott Tel: 01732 884023.

- *Overseas Jobs Express*, a twice monthly newspaper, carries TEFL vacancies. For subscription enquiries, contact 01273 699611 (subscription costs are £39 for three months; £70 for six months). Website: www.overseasjobsexpress.co.uk

- TEFL jobs are usually advertised in the education section of *The Guardian* on Tuesdays and the *Times Educational Supplement* on Fridays.

- For opportunities of teaching opportunities with the British Council, which operate a network of English language teaching centres in over 50 developing countries, look at their website, which carries a vacancies section: www.britishcouncil.org

- Schools running TEFL courses are often notified of TEFL jobs abroad.

The rest of this section lists some of the main organisations recruiting paid teachers of English as a foreign language.

Central Bureau for International Education and Training

The Central Bureau is the UK agency for the development of an international dimension in education and training. It offers information and professional advice on educational exchanges and administers international programmes and professional development activities. The Bureau's services enhance the quality of learning provision, especially in the areas of foreign languages and communications.

English Language Assistants Programme

This programme places UK students and teachers in schools and colleges abroad. The role of the assistant is to help the teacher of

English and, in particular, to help improve pupils' spoken and listening skills, and to present aspects of the English-speaking culture they represent. The assistantship also provides an opportunity to acquire skills such as language skills, cultural awareness, presentation skills and people management. Graduates and undergraduates of any discipline, who are aged 20-30, native speakers of English and who have a knowledge of the relevant language at least to A level or equivalent, can apply. Modern language undergraduates can take a year out as a language assistant after two years of their degree.

Placements are available in Central/Eastern Europe (no language requirement), France, Belgium, Quebec, Germany, Italy, Spain and Latin America. Priority is given to undergraduates for placements in Italy and Spain and application is usually made via the university. Application should be made between October and 1st December in the year prior to the placement although late applications may be accepted. Placements usually start in Sept/October and last for the academic year.

Contact: The Central Bureau, The British Council, 10 Spring Gardens, London SW1A 2BN.

Tel: 020 7389 4596. Fax: 020 7389 4594.

Email: assistants@britishcouncil.org

Website: www.britishcouncil.org/cbiet/assistants/

Council on International Educational Exchange (Council Exchanges)

Council Exchanges, a registered UK charitable trust, offers a variety of work placement abroad programmes (described elsewhere in this chapter) and opportunities for teaching English, described below.

The JET Programme - teach in Japan

Sponsored by the Japanese Government, the Japan Exchange and Teaching (JET) Programme offers one-year teaching contracts to graduates with an interest in Japanese culture, to assist in teaching English. There are over 6000 JET participants from over 39 countries currently working in Japan; in 2001, 732 were British graduates. Participants must hold a UK passport, must not be aged over 35, nor have lived in Japan for three out of the past ten years. Council Exchanges provides advice from former participants, handbooks and language books and tapes, as well as orientations in London and Tokyo, working visa and return flights to Japan and assistance and support services in Japan.

Teach in China, Teach in Thailand

Teach in China provides five- and ten-month renewable contracts teaching English at universities and colleges throughout China. Teach in Thailand is a similar programme which offers teaching placements at Thai primary and secondary schools. Graduates of any disciplines, as well as current and retired teachers, are eligible for the programme. Teaching qualifications are not required, as a TEFL training session is provided in Beijing and Bangkok. Accommodation and local salary are also provided.

Contact: Council Exchanges, 52 Poland Street, London W1V 4JQ.

Tel: 020 7478 2020. Fax: 020 7478 7322.

Email: infoUK@councilexchanges.org.uk

Website: www.councilexchanges.org.uk

International House

International House is a large independent employer of TEFL staff, with over 120 affiliated schools in 34 countries.

Contact: International House, 106 Piccadilly, London W1J 7NL.

Tel: 020 7518 6999. Fax: 020 7518 6998.

Email: info@inlondon.co.uk

Website: www.inlondon.com

Profile   Andrea Birch
Teaching English as a foreign language

'It was really my German tutor at university who first got me interested in taking a year out after my degree, and teaching English abroad. (I was studying English, and German was my first-year subsidiary course). I decided that as soon as I had completed my degree, I would enrol on a TEFL course. It was an excellent four-week course (equivalent to the RSA certificate). There was a brilliant sense of team spirit in the group which made the work very interesting and extremely enjoyable.

When the course finished I was a little apprehensive about going abroad immediately and decided to gain more experience on a summer school course. I was offered a teaching post in Manchester, which I thoroughly enjoyed. As I was soon to discover, these types of courses are very different from teaching abroad as they not only require a lot of energy and enthusiasm inside the classroom but outside, too! As a summer teacher I also accompanied students on excursions, sports afternoons, and even to discos! Summer courses are designed to immerse the students in the English language and culture, and as a teacher it was my responsibility to make their stay as enjoyable as possible. It was an exhausting but equally rewarding experience and something I eagerly applied to do after my year abroad.

In September I was ready to take up the challenge of doing something completely different and chose to go to Greece for the following ten months. I was situated on the mainland in a remote town called Agrinio. Tourists were an alien concept in this part of the country and I soon realised that my English presence would instantly attract piercing stares from many of the Greek locals. However, I didn't mind this too much as it was all part of the challenge of living in a different country.

My employers were lovely and really looked after me well. Wherever you go just make sure you have a contract that you are happy to sign and you take lots of insect repellent! The winter was surprisingly cold. (So if Greece appeals don't just think sun-cream is all you'll need.)

I had about twenty-six hours' teaching a week, and taught complete beginners to First Certificate level. The students were aged between seven and eighteen and were put into classes according to their ability and age. It was very impressive to see how eager the majority of students were to learn English - particularly the younger ones - and how quickly they progressed.

Teaching in Greece doesn't pay that well, but I had enough money to travel and have a good social life. I made good friends - English teachers and local Greek people.

I enjoyed my year so much that I wanted to pursue TEFL further and since returning to England I have taught in a Japanese College, and am now working as an Education and Recruitment Officer, which involves writing educational material and recruiting teachers for summer and overseas work.

To teach English as a foreign language is not an easy thing to do, and requires a great deal of enthusiasm and commitment both to the English language and to the students under your care and supervision.

I would say to anyone thinking about taking a year out, who thinks they have the necessary qualities and can meet the challenge, to seriously consider teaching English as a foreign language - you never know where it could take you.'

Club de Relaciones Culturales Internacionales

As part of its programmes, described earlier in this chapter, this organisation runs a language assistant programme, where you live with a family, assisting and tutoring the family in English for 15 hrs/ week.

Contact: Club de Relaciones Culturales Internacionales, Departmento Socio-Cultural, Ferraz, 82, 28008 Madrid, Spain.

Tel: 00 34 1 541 71 03.

Working in the tourist industry

The tourist industry worldwide recruits many seasonal and short-term contract staff. Opportunities include the following:

- working on campsites/at holiday centres
- entertaining and organising children on activity holidays and summer camps in the USA
- hotel work - being a waiter/waitress, room attendant, etc
- working in a ski resort - as chalet staff
- tour guide/courier
- resort representative work
- working in restaurants/bars/cafés, etc.

Knowledge of a foreign language is essential for some positions, and applicants usually need to be at least 18, or, for some positions, older. Tour companies look for evidence of maturity and experience of dealing with the public.

As well as the opportunities listed below, some of the organisations mentioned earlier in this chapter which offer wide-ranging work placement programmes, such as Council Exchanges and Changing Worlds, can help you to access job opportunities related to the tourist industry.

BUNAC – Summer Camp USA

BUNAC operates a variety of opportunities for paid work abroad; their work/travel programmes are described earlier in this chapter. Summer Camp USA and KAMP are their programmes offering the opportunity to work on children's summer camps in the USA.

Summer Camp USA requires students, and non-students, between the ages of 19 and 35 to work as camp counsellors on children's summer camps in America from June to mid/end August. Working as a counsellor may mean teaching, supervising an activity or acting as a confidential adviser to the children. A registration fee of £62 is required. Summer Camp USA finds placements for suitable applicants and arranges return flights, visa and insurance. Camps provide board and lodging and a salary of $565-$625. Applicants must be energetic and hard-working, and have some previous experience of working with groups of children.

KAMP (Kitchen and Maintenance Programme) is open to students currently in higher education (or an appropriate level catering course). It offers the chance to undertake a number of non-counselling jobs on summer camps, including food preparation, maintenance, administration and laundry. Air fares and insurance are paid for. The cost of registration is £62.

Contact: BUNAC, 16 Bowling Green Lane, London EC1R 0QH.

Tel: 020 7251 3472. Fax: 020 7251 0215.

Website: www.bunac.org.uk

Camp America

Camp America arranges for young people (18+) to work on US summer camps or at American resorts for nine weeks, either as counsellors (looking after children) or as camp workers (working in the kitchen, laundry, office, etc). Camp America offers free return flight, meals and accommodation, pocket money and up to ten weeks for independent travel.

Apply as early as you can. Applicants must be available from 1 June. Approximately 10,000 people are recruited annually.

Contact: Camp America, Department AYO, 37a Queen's Gate, London SW7 5HR.

Tel: 020 7581 7373.

Website: www.campamerica.co.uk

Email: brochure@campamerica.co.uk

Camp Counselors USA & Work Experience USA and Down Under

Apart from the Work Experience programmes described earlier in this chapter, this organisation offers Camp Counselors USA. Camp Counselors USA work with over 850 summer camps in America. They have a 100% placement record, and have placed over 60,000 people in the last 15 years.

Contact: Camp Counselors USA & Work Experience USA and Down Under, Green Dragon House, 64-70 High Street, Croydon, Surrey CR0 9XN.

Tel: 020 8688 9051. Fax: 020 8681 8168.

Email: inquiry@ccusaweusa.co.uk

Website: www.campcounselors.com or www.workexperienceusa.com

Canvas Holidays Ltd

Canvas Holidays Ltd employ hard-working, flexible and friendly individuals and couples to work mainly as campsite couriers (putting up and taking down tents, meeting and greeting customers, problem solving), children's couriers (organisation and supervision of children's activities and general courier duties) and wildlife guides (organisation and supervision of wildlife walks and activities, and general courier duties). The work is based on luxury campsites mainly in France but also in Austria, Germany, Luxembourg, Spain, Italy and Switzerland. Some supervisory positions are also available – experience of working within the camping industry is essential.

Applicants must be 19 years or over and, ideally, available from the end of March – mid October and must have had experience of dealing with the public. A working knowledge of a major European language is preferred but not essential. The salary is £98 per week. Tented accommodation, uniform and medical cover is also provided.

Contact: Overseas Personnel Coordinator, Canvas Holidays Ltd, East Port House, 12 East Port, Dunfermline, Fife KY12 7JG.

Tel: 01383 629018. Fax: 01383 629071.

Website: www.canvasholidays.com

Carisma Holidays Ltd

Opportunities are available to work on beach sites on the west coast of France, taking responsibility for client families. Duties include welcoming families, providing information and advice, cleaning and maintaining mobile homes and baby sitting. Applicants should be aged 19+, be EU nationals, have a helpful and friendly disposition, and experience of dealing with people. Full season couriers work from May to the end of September; high season couriers from July to the end of September. Wages are £70-£100 per week, according to the position. Accommodation is provided and travel to and from the resort is paid. Full training is given. Apply from October onwards.

Contact: Carisma Holidays Ltd, Bethel House, Heronsgate Road, Chorleywood, Herts WD3 5BB.

Tel: 01923 284235. Fax: 01923 284560.

Email: info@carisma.co.uk

Website: www.carisma.co.uk

Esprit Holidays Ltd

Through their Esprit Ski and Esprit Alpine Sun programmes, Esprit holidays offer winter and summer seasonal work in resorts in France, Italy, Austria, Switzerland, USA and Canada. Opportunities exist for chalet hosts and kids' club leaders. Applicants must be 18 or over. Full training is given, so an interest in cooking or working with children is the only requirement. Relevant experience, however, is an advantage and the company look for enthusiastic, positive people, with a desire to provide high levels of customer care. Staff are employed for between four and six months; apply at any time of the year. Staff receive a wage, accommodation, board, ski hire and ski pass (winter only). Full insurance is included.

Contact: Esprit Holidays Ltd, 185 Fleet Road, Fleet, Hampshire GU51 3BL.
Tel: 01252 618318. Fax: 01252 618328.
Email: recruitment@esprit-holidays.co.uk
Website: esprit-holidays.co.uk

Eurocamp plc

Eurocamp plc employs over 1,500 overseas staff every summer to work on campsites in 12 European countries. Staff are expected to provide excellent customer service at all times to holidaymakers, who stay in tents or holiday homes, where everything is provided. There is a variety of positions available including courier, children's courier and montage/demontage assistants. Montage assistants are needed early in the season to put up the tents and get the equipment ready; demontage assistants work late in the season taking down the tents and putting the equipment into store. Applicants do not need languages for these two positions; they just need to be physically strong. Other positions require different skills and abilities. However, most require a good working knowledge of one other major European language. Applicants must be aged 18 or over, and available from April/May to September/October.

Contact: Overseas Recruitment Department, Eurocamp Summer Jobs (Ref YO), PO Box 170, Liverpool L70 1ES.
Tel: 01606 787522.

Profile **Charlotte Goldsmith**

From ski chalets to tents - with First Choice and Eurocamp

'Because medicine is such a long course, I decided to take time out and have some fun before the hard work really began! Another reason why I knew a year out would be good for me was that I was taking my A levels a year early, so would have been quite young to go to medical school. The majority of the interviewers at medical school thought a year out was a good idea - as long as you could explain why it was right for you.

I worked in an office until December to earn some money before I went to work in the French Alps as a waitress/chambermaid for First Choice/Skibound - basically so that I could do as much skiing as possible. I was very nervous at first, but by the second day it already felt like home. The pay is bad (just enough to survive on!) and the hours are long and hard, but there is this amazing sense of team spirit, and everyone is always up for a wild night out!

Some of the people you work with may not be the type you would normally be friendly with, but you learn to get along and by the end of the season you realise what great friends you've become. There are times when you fall out, so you learn how to compromise as everyone has their own opinion on certain things.

I then went to work for Eurocamp in the summer as a courier on a campsite. I had to clean all the accommodation and do all the paperwork. It was a good experience, as I had a lot of responsibility. I learned how to deal with customers, and it was an ideal opportunity to improve my French. Living in a tent for five months is an experience in itself, and I would recommend it to anyone! There was a big crowd of us and we had beach parties and made good use of the bar - there was never a dull moment! I had such an amazing time that I'm going back to work for Eurocamp again this summer.

It was very strange coming back to medical school, and getting back into studying did get some getting used to. But I'm now so independent and used to looking after myself, that being away from home is not a problem for me as it is for some students, and I definitely have some stories to share with people!'

French Encounters

French Encounters is a specialist schools tour operator, organising educational language field trips for children aged 10-13. The week-long field trips are based in two châteaux in Normandy. Eight animateurs/animatrices are recruited annually, to help run the programmes and to be role models for the children. The work includes preparing equipment and activities, accompanying the children on excursions, organising indoor/outdoor activities and evening entertainments, and encouraging the children to speak French. Applicants should be aged 18-22, with French A level (or the equivalent) with good oral skills. Experience of working with children aged 10-13 is useful. Applicants should also have enthusiasm, good organisational and social skills and the ability to work as part of a team. A two-week training period is provided with regular further training, including First Aid and presentation skills. Employment is for four months, mid-February to mid-June. Apply before 31st August. Full board and lodging, travel and insurance are provided. Approximately FF600 per week pocket money is paid.

Directrices, responsible for the management of each centre, are also required annually for temporary full-time contracts. Ideal for females (exempt from the Sex Discrimination Act) with a degree in French, or those taking a career break or early retirement.

Contact: French Encounters, 63 Fordhouse Road, Bromsgrove, Worcestershire B60 2LU.

Tel: 01527 873645. Fax: 01527 832794.

Email: admin@frenchencounters.freeserve.co.uk

Website: www.frenchencounters.co.uk

Innovative Cruise Services

Innovative Cruise Services are consultants to the cruise industry. The industry is booming at the moment with many new ships being put into service creating thousands of jobs in all departments. The requirements are that you must be over 19 years of age with experience in the position applied for. Contracts are usually for three to six months and are renewable. Registration fee, which includes a 270-page career guide and two years' supply of newsletters containing vacany lists, is £26.

Contact: Innovative Cruise Services, 36 Midlothian Drive, Glasgow G14 3QU.

Tel: 0141 649 8644. Fax: 0141 636 1016

Email: info@cruiseservices.co.uk

Website: www.cruiseservices.co.uk

Jobs in the Alps

Jobs in the Alps is an agency which places British workers in mountain resorts in France, Germany and Switzerland for the winter and summer seasons. Applicants for jobs come from a variety of backgrounds; some have worked in hotels, offices, factories, etc and others apply before, during and after university. Most applicants need a reasonable knowledge of French or German.

The positions for which there are vacancies include waiting, buffet and kitchen staff, hall porters and night porters, housekeepers, receptionists, bar staff, cashiers and cleaners in hotels, restaurants, mountain restaurants and cafés and occasional au pair work in families.

Most winter jobs start early to mid-December and last until mid-April; there are a few in January when replacements may be needed. Most summer jobs are for three months, from mid/end June to mid/end September. Workers must commit themselves to the whole season.

All employees have free board and lodging. They are entitled to cheap lift passes and cheap travel. Employees work about 45 hours a week, usually with two free days. The pay ranges between £120 and £150 (less for au pair work) a week depending on the job.

Applicants must be a least 18 and work experience will be required for some positions. For some jobs, language skills are essential; for others, such as backroom jobs, this will be less important. Approximately 200 people are sent to jobs for the winter season and 150 people for the summer. Early application for all positions is highly recommended (by mid-September for winter positions and by mid-April for summer positions).

Contact (enclosing SAE): Jobs in the Alps, 17 High Street, Gretton, Northamptonshire NN17 3DE.

Tel: 01536 771150.

Email: jobs@jobs-in-the-alps.com

Website: www.jobs-in-the-alps.com

NST Travel Group Plc

NST Travel Group are an educational travel company, which has been operating for over 30 years. Employment opportunities are available at their activity centres in the south of France, and in the UK. They also have opportunities in northern France at their centre running language and educational courses. Positions available include: activity and ICT instructors, multi-activity instructors, French speaking group coordinators, entertainment organisers, catering staff, drivers, bar staff and cleaning/maintenance staff. Staff are taken on for a minimum of two months, and a maximum of a full season - 11 months. There are no particular requirements, although the organisation looks for people who are flexible and happy to work as a team, and who will play their part in ensuring that the guests have a memorable stay.

Staff gain experience in working with children and/or in outdoor pursuits. Training is provided, and their are opportunities to gain recognised awards and qualifications. Apply from September - December. Accommodation is provided, at a small charge. Staff employed in France are paid a competitive wage; UK staff are paid at the National Minimum Wage rate.

Contact: NST Travel Group Plc, Chiltern House, Bristol Avenue, Blackpool FY2 0FA.

Tel: 01253 503011. Fax: 01253 356955.

Email: nst@nstgroup.co.uk

Website: www.nstjobs.co.uk

PGL Travel Ltd

PGL Travel Ltd recruits staff to work at residential activity centres in the UK, France and Spain. There are vacancies for outdoor activity instructors, for group leaders (responsible for the organisation and welfare of children) and for various support roles. The latter include kitchen staff, drivers, nurses, maintenance and domestic staff. Couriers are also recruited to accompany children on trips to various parts of Europe. Please see the PGL section in chapter 6 for more detailed information.

Contact: Personnel Department, PGL Travel Ltd, Alton Court, Penyard Lane, Ross-on Wye, Herefordshire HR9 5GL.

Tel: 01989 767833. Fax: 01989 768769.

Email: personnel@pgl.co.uk

Website: www.pgl.co.uk/personnel

Village Camps

Village Camps have organised educational and activity camps for international children for 30 years. During the summer, camps are based in Switzerland, Austria and France. During the winter, ski and snowboard programmes are run in Switzerland, and outdoor education programmes in the spring and autumn. Staff are recruited to run activities for the children and to supervise them on camp. Domestic and administration staff are also recruited. Staff are recruited for 3-8 weeks. An allowance is provided, plus accommodation and board. Staff are responsible for their own travel and insurance costs. The minimum age for domestic staff is 18, for programme staff (to work with children) is 21. For summer camps, apply in March; for the winter season apply in September, and for spring camps, apply in January.

Contact: Village Camps, 14 rue de la Morâche, 1260 Nyon, Switzerland.

Tel: 00 41 22 990 9405. Fax: 00 41 22 990 9494

Email: personnel@villagecamps.ch

Website: www.villagecamps.com

World Challenge Expeditions

This organisation runs a variety of challenging and developmental programmes overseas, for those aged 16-24, described in chapter 13. Their Gap Challenge programme offers opportunities for paid placements, such as hotel work in Canada.

Contact: World Challenge Expeditions, Black Arrow House, 2 Chandos Road, London NW10 6NF. Tel: 020 8728 7272.

Email: welcome@world-challenge.co.uk

Website: www.world-challenge.co.uk

WorldNetUK

WorldNetUK offers a camp USA programme, working as a camp counsellor, for which you need to be aged at least 19 years by 1 June, and available for eight to ten weeks from June. You must be fluent in

English, and be a student, teacher, youth worker or someone with specialised skills e.g. in soccer, swimming, outdoor pursuits, arts and crafts etc.

Contact: WorldNetUK, Emberton House, 26 Shakespeare Road, Bedford MK40 2ED.

Tel: 07002 287247 (for a brochure). Fax: 01234 351070.

Email: info@worldnetuk.com

Website: www.worldnetuk.com

Undertaking a career-related work placement during (or shortly after) your higher education course

Organisations listed in this section offer opportunities particularly to students while undertaking higher education, or recent graduates. This enables students to gain some work experience relevant to their chosen career.

Council on International Educational Exchange (Council Exchanges)

Besides the various programmes described elsewhere in this chapter, Council Exchanges offers opportunities for students and recent graduates to undertake career-related work placements.

Internship Canada

The Internship Canada programme gives participants the opportunity to take a work placement anywhere in Canada for up to twelve months. This programme is ideal for students who require practical experience as part of their course, and is open to full-time students at the HND level or above, as well as gap-year students with an unconditional offer. Participants are required to find their own placement, and can start at any time of year. Council Exchanges can supply information and advice on how to find a placement in Canada.

Internship USA

Internship USA enables students and recent graduates to work in the US for up to eighteen months in a position directly related to their studies and future careers. Full-time students at the HND level or above are eligible, as are graduates who start their internship within twelve months of completing their course. Council Exchanges can provide information and advice on how to find an internship in the States, as well as access to a searchable database of internships through the Council Exchanges website. Once participants have secured their placement in the US, Council Exchanges acts as legal sponsor to get the necessary visa for working in the USA.

Internship New Zealand

Internship New Zealand allows participants to work for up to six months in New Zealand, with the possibility to extend their stay for a further six months. Council Exchanges offers an internship placement service and advice and assistance when in New Zealand. The programme is open to students or recent graduates with UK citizenship.

Contact: Council Exchanges, 52 Poland Street, London W1V 4JQ.

Tel: 020 7478 2020. Fax: 020 7478 7322

Email: infoUK@councilexchanges.org.uk

Website: www.councilexchanges.org.uk

IAESTE

The International Association for the Exchange of Students for Technical Experience (IAESTE) is an independent worldwide organisation for which the Central Bureau for International Education and Training is the UK office. IAESTE provides course-related paid work experience placements abroad for science, agriculture, horticulture, architecture, engineering and computer science students. Over 80 countries are members of IAESTE and, since 1948 over 270,000 students have gained work experience through the programme.

Most placements are from six to twelve weeks from June to September (some placements can be up to a year) and students at British universities who are interested in the scheme need to apply to Central Bureau from September to December in the year before they would like to do their work experience. There is a placement fee of £48.

Students taking part in the programme are usually in their second or third year of higher education. IAESTE national offices find accommodation for incoming students and students receive a salary while they are working. Students do, however, have to pay their air fare and insurance.

Contact: IAESTE at Central Bureau for International Education and Training, 10 Spring Gardens, London SW1A 2BN.

Tel: 020 7389 4774. Fax: 020 7389 4426.

Email: iaeste@britishcouncil.org

Website: www.iaeste.org.uk

Leonardo da Vinci

Leonardo da Vinci is a European Community programme which provides opportunities for higher education students and recent graduates to undertake periods of vocational training with companies in other European countries, for between three and twelve months. The Leonardo programme cannot pay you a salary, as this is up to individual employers to decide, but can make a contribution to the cost of language tuition and some day-to-day expenses.

Contact: The Central Bureau for International Education and Training, The British Council, 10 Spring Gardens, London SW1A 2BN.

Tel: 020 7389 4389.

Website: www.leonardo.org.uk

N.B. Under the Socrates-Erasmus programme, it is possible to spend part of your higher education course studying in another European country. For further details, see chapter 11.

For further information on EU programmes related to higher education, consult the DfES booklet *The European Choice - A Guide to Opportunities for Higher Education in Europe*, available in careers centres or from DfES Publications Centre tel: 0845 60 222 60, or email dfes@prologistics.co.uk (listing reference EC/2001).

Chapter 10
Voluntary work abroad

Many organisations offer you the opportunity to undertake activities abroad which enable you to contribute to the community.

Organisations offering 'voluntary' work vary considerably in financial arrangements with the volunteer. For most opportunities, you will incur some costs yourself, if only travel expenses, but some organisations require a considerable contribution from you. The common element, however, in all the opportunities listed in this chapter is that they will be of interest to any of you wanting to give your time and energy to something which you feel is a worthwhile cause, in Europe or worldwide.

The majority of opportunities described in this chapter do not require specific occupational skills or experience, and generally some training/orientation is provided. A few organisations are specifically looking for volunteers with professional skills and experience. The majority of organisations recruit people aged 18 and over; sometimes there is a maximum age limit of, for example, 25 or older.

Questions to ask yourself

- What sort of work do I want to do?
- Which area of the world do I want to go to?
- How long a placement am I looking for?
- What are the financial implications?

- What level of support is offered?
- How can I maximise my chances of being accepted?

What sort of work?

There is a huge range of different kinds of experience available. They fall into the following broad categories:

- opportunities for working on social projects/with people in need - includes social and community projects such as working with disadvantaged children, assisting or teaching in schools, working with people with disabilities, or the elderly. Other opportunities involve working on health projects, technical work, or on practical projects. Many organisations sending volunteers abroad concentrate on voluntary projects in the more deprived and poorer areas of the world. Volunteers are usually recruited for several months to two years, and are the only volunteer on placement in the community, or they may be placed together with one or two other volunteers. Some organisations in this category look particularly for volunteers with occupational skills and experience. (**Organisations offering this kind of opportunity are coded S in individual descriptions later in this chapter.**)

- environmental and conservation work - includes ecological fieldwork, practical conservation work, such as clearing land, replanting forestry, building work, etc, through to working on archaeological projects. While most of the work is practical, there may also be the opportunity for undertaking administrative work. Usually no experience is required and training is given. (**Organisations offering this kind of opportunity are denoted by C in individual organisations' descriptions later in this chapter.**)

- participating in short-term workcamps - working with a group of other volunteers on workcamps lasting from one to four weeks. The work is often practical, such as building, gardening, general maintenance, undertaking conservation projects, or community projects. (**Organisations offering this kind of opportunity are denoted by W in individual organisations' descriptions later in this chapter.**)

- working on a kibbutz - a rural communal settlement in Israel, where work, income and property are shared by its members. As a working visitor on a kibbutz, you experience and contribute to this particular kind of community organisation. (**Organisations offering this kind of opportunity are denoted by K in individual organisations' descriptions later in this chapter.**)

Where in the world?

Some of you will have a specific country or continent in mind. If not, you need to consider whether you wish to spend time in a westernised, industrialised society, or in a developing country, where living conditions and the culture are likely to be very different from those in the UK. Do as much research as you can to find out about any countries of interest - read, talk to people who know the area and so on.

Organisations sending volunteers to a number of countries will usually allow you to state a preference for your destination country. They have to match the wishes and experience of the applicants with available opportunities, of course. You are more likely to find a suitable placement if you are prepared to be flexible about your destination.

How long for?

Opportunities available vary, from as little as a week to up to two years. You need to think about the duration of your placement in relation to your overall plan for your 'time out', as discussed in chapter 1. Do you want to do several different things in your gap year? How well do you want to get to know the country and community where you will be going? Obviously the longer you are on your voluntary placement, the better you get to know the people and area. Do you want to build time for travelling around into your year? If so, you will need to choose a project with placement periods that allow time for this - either before or after your placement.

If you need to raise funds beforehand, you will need to make sure you have enough time for this. If you are taking a gap year before higher education, the time available for fundraising in the final months of your last year at school or college will be limited. Perhaps you will need to look at opportunities which allow a little breathing space after exams to raise some finances.

What are the financial implications?

Obviously a question of prime importance! You need to consider travel and insurance, food and accommodation costs, personal spending money, visas etc. Which of these, if any, are paid for by the organisation? Which will you have to fund yourself?

Some organisations require the volunteer to make a considerable financial contribution to cover the costs of their placement, air fares etc, sometimes in the region of £2,000 or more. At the other end of the scale, a few organisations, such as VSO, pay volunteers remuneration equivalent to the local rate for the job, and travel expenses. This is more typical for organisations recruiting skilled and experienced staff. In between, there are varying arrangements: some

121

provide accommodation but you have to pay your travel expenses; for some, volunteers pay all their costs; or volunteers pay a registration fee, but are provided with accommodation and an allowance as pocket money.

Plan your finances carefully, and don't underestimate how much you will need! Chapter 3 provides further general advice about finances, finding sponsorship and fundraising. Contact individual organisations for specific information and advice.

What level of support is offered?

Do not overlook this important aspect, particularly if you intend to go to a remote or rural setting, and/or will be working independently rather than alongside other volunteers. Health, welfare and security organisations, for example, can operate quite differently in other countries. Having access to good quality back-up and support if you need it can be crucial. This is especially vital if your communication skills in the local languages are limited. Good quality support is important not only if you are in a developing country, but also within Europe; the culture and level of development is very different, for example, in many Eastern European countries from our own.

- Is there an agent or representative of the organisation in the country?

- What happens if there are problems and difficulties with your placement?

- How much contact will you have with other volunteers?

- Is accommodation provided, or do you have to find your own?

- In an emergency, how easily can you get home?

- Whose responsibility is it to organise health and other kinds of insurance?

- What back-up is there in the event of serious illness?

Think about the level of back-up and support that you feel you need, and then look at what is provided with opportunities of interest. Try to talk to past volunteers about their experiences - most organisations can put you in touch with people.

Maximising your chances!

All organisations expect volunteers to be committed to the project they apply for. Some of the organisations sending volunteers on longer-term programmes have fairly rigorous application procedures. They will be looking particularly to see if you have the personal qualities and skills that they feel their volunteers require. You need to have thought through your reasons for wanting to do voluntary work, why you have applied to their organisation, and what you hope to achieve from the experience.

The organisation will expect you to have done enough initial research to show that you have a realistic idea of what they offer. Tell them about any similar voluntary work you have done before. Mention any positions of responsibility you have held, and give examples that show you can work both as part of a team and independently. If you have visited the parts of the world where you hope to go, make sure the organisation knows that you already have some familiarity with the area.

And finally...

Undertaking a period of voluntary work in a different country is a challenging way of spending your time out. However long or short, it not only allows you to make a small contribution to other societies, but offers you the chance to gain personally in many ways.

You will learn more about yourself, and develop personal and other skills. You will learn about another country and culture, make new friends, and, as many organisations recruit volunteers from all over the world, you may get to know people of many nationalities. Undertaking voluntary work also helps to enhance your CV.

The personal accounts given in this chapter from past volunteers speak for themselves, showing how much people gain from their experiences. Be prepared for the experience to affect your life!

Listings of organisations

The remainder of this chapter comprises descriptions of voluntary opportunities provided by over fifty organisations. These are listed alphabetically. To help you locate opportunities of interest to you, entries have been coded as follows:

C = environmental and conservation work - includes practical conservation work and archaeological projects

K = working on a kibbutz

S = working on social projects/with people in need - includes working with young people, assisting/teaching in schools, working with people with disabilities, or the elderly. Also includes health projects, technical work, or other practical projects

W = short-term workcamps - working with a group of other volunteers on workcamps for one to four weeks. The work is often practical, such as building, gardening, maintenance etc

EXP = occupational skills and experience preferred or required for some/all projects. Such organisations could be of particular interest to those with established careers who wish to take a career break.

Africa & Asia Venture $\qquad$ **S**

Africa & Asia Venture provides hard-working school/college leavers who want to spend time in Africa - in Kenya, Tanzania, Botswana, Uganda or Malawi - and in Northern India or Nepal with constructive and rewarding work experience combined with companionship, travel and adventure.

Volunteers are placed in pairs as assistant teachers in selected schools for one term. Depending on their skills and attributes, they assist in a variety of subjects ranging from English, sciences, music and vocational activities to clubs and sports. Schools are chosen with location, work opportunities, accommodation and security in mind and placements do not deprive local teachers of work. There are also opportunities for attachments to do conservation community-related projects in Kenya.

Placements are usually for four months, departing September, early January or late April. Following the placement, volunteers have two weeks for independent travel and the complete programme is rounded off with a group safari to places of interest such as Lake Turkana, Victoria Falls, Rajasthan or the Himalayas.

Volunteers should be a minimum of 17¾ and should be studying A levels, or the equivalent, and intending to go on to further study. They must be highly motivated, in good health and interested in working with young people of other cultures. There are also a few vacancies for graduates.

The cost for applicants is approximately £2300, which covers comprehensive health and personal effects insurance, orientation, training and in-country back-up, living allowance commensurate with local wages, self-catering accommodation, all-inclusive safari and a contribution towards educating an overseas child. It does not cover the return air fare or extra spending money. Africa & Asia Venture gives advice on raising funds.

Applicants should apply early, as placements get booked up. Applicants will then be invited to an interview where their suitability will be assessed. Those selected attend an orientation course on arrival overseas.

Contact: Africa & Asia Venture, 10 Market Place, Devizes, Wiltshire SN10 1HT
Tel: 01380 729009. Fax: 01380 72006
Email: av@aventure.co.uk
Website: www.aventure.co.uk

Profile   **Rebecca Scott**
Teaching in Nepal with Africa & Asia Venture

'I really don't know where to start summing up the best experiences of my life – it's hard to convey to you on paper all the anxiety, excitement, sadness, laughter and pure enjoyment of my 'gap year'.

I survived my A levels but I was sick of the education system. I wanted to do something different before starting university. I wanted an adventure in which the intrinsic enjoyment would outweigh any sort of end result. And that's certainly what I got.

After a few boring weeks in the local Sainsburys, I spent the next three months in sunny San Francisco. I had an amazing time cramming in as much as I possibly could – Disneyland, L.A, Hollywood, Lake Tahoe, Mexico, lectures at Berkley University, sight seeing, boat trips, bike rides and swimming. I also worked as a receptionist, a wallpaper hanger and finally, for one and a half months, covering the houses of wealthy Californians with Christmas fairy lights.

I returned to good old Blighty and the comfort of my family for Christmas, and found myself behind that checkout at Sainsburys for another two weeks. Then in January I boarded a plane for Nepal along with 29 strangers all on their gap year. We were about to embark on three months teaching in remote Nepali schools. My placement was arranged by Africa & Asia Venture, a company I would recommend to anyone thinking of taking up some voluntary teaching work abroad.

Although it was hard work getting the funds for my placement, this pales into insignificance when 1 remember my time spent in beautiful Nepal. The teaching wasn't easy; you try controlling a class of 78 six-year-olds! Really, it was hugely rewarding. I will never forget the people I met out there, both Nepalese and other English volunteers. The things I saw and did have left a lasting imprint on my mind. These experiences ranged from watching the sunrise over the Himalayas to taking part in a nationwide water fight. From holding a 4-hour-old baby to milking a buffalo. From being the first white person a group of villagers had ever seen to riding on the roof of a bus for eight-hour stretches after trips to Kathmandu. From white water rafting to hiding in the grass just metres away from a rhino. Even now, sitting in my room at university, I get a pang of homesickness thinking of the people and places I left behind.

After I bid my tearful goodbye to Nepal, I headed on for a month of backpacking heaven in Thailand.

The most amazing thing about travelling for me, was how empowered I felt – the sense of total freedom is something I can't compare to any other period of my life. At the end of all this, I was definitely ready to *start university. My time away served to remind me why it is that I want to learn. I've caught the travel bug big time, but I'm not going to sacrifice the opportunity to further my education and meet more amazing people here at university.'*

Profile   **Sarah Chase**

To Kenya with Africa & Asia Venture

'*After weeks of wading through Gap Year brochures and newspaper cuttings, I finally found one which immediately stood out. Set up by Africa Venture, it involved teaching for three months in a remote secondary boarding school in Kenya, followed by a month of free time to head off backpacking independently.*

A year later I was sitting on a Kenyan Airways flight bound for Nairobi with the other 23 members of the group. After a week's orientation course, we were sent off in pairs to the schools we would be teaching at, all in Western Kenya. Fortunately, Debbie, my partner, and I hit it off immediately and soon settled in to the daily life at the school. We were made to feel most welcome from day one, with frequent invitations to the other teachers' houses for sweet milky Kenyan tea to which we soon became completely addicted.

I began teaching French, English and History to forms one and two, which related to years 9 and 10 in English schools although it wasn't unusual to find girls of 18 or older, as some had started school so late due to illness or family money problems. The school had just 200 girls and very few textbooks - just five between the 55 girls in my English class, which was quite tough for them but I tried to incorporate activities which didn't rely on books. Naturally, this sometimes became quite noisy, although I was very impressed at how keen they were to get involved and learn as much as possible. In a country with frequent reports of corruption and crime, the girls frequently had ambitions to be doctors or lawyers in the belief that the youth will be able to change things. As many of the girls came from tiny huts in the hills from families with eight or more children, and whose parents often couldn't speak much English or even Kiswahili, the other national language, themselves, I was struck by their determination and hope.

At times we were taken aback by their lack of knowledge, and soon realised that they understood very little about the developed world. After writing down a list of important inventions in the last fifty years during a history lesson, I then had to spend two more lessons explaining what the inventions were, such as computers, satellites and even dishwashers as so many of the girls had no idea what they were, or their relevance to everyday life. As our village had no electricity and only very occasional running water, I could understand why this was so. However, being able to share such different cultures and customs was as fascinating to us as it was to the girls and teachers at the school, and provided endless hours of amusement for us all.

The term seemed to fly by and before we knew it, end-of-term exams were looming and we were saying our goodbyes. I'll definitely keep in touch with the friends I made there and hope that some will fulfil their ambitions - they deserve to.'

AFS International Youth Development   S

Opportunities for 18-29 year-olds to spend six months in Latin America and South Africa living with a volunteer host family, and working alongside local people on community social projects, dealing with issues such as health, education, the environment, community development and working with underprivileged children and people with disabilities.

Contact: AFS International Youth Development, Leeming House, Vicar Lane, Leeds LS2 7JF.

Tel: 0845 458 2101. Fax: 0845 458 2102.

Email: info-unitedkingdom@afs.org

Website: www.afsuk.org

Archaeology Abroad   C/W

Volunteers - usual minimum age 18 - are required for periods of from two weeks to three months for a range of outdoor tasks, including surveying, field-walking, excavation and small finds processing. Food and basic communal accommodation are often provided, but volunteers pay own fares and occasionally a registration fee. Conditions may be sparse in rural locations.

Archaeology Abroad offers a limited number of Fieldwork Awards of between £100-200 towards the cost of participating in a project listed in its bulletins. All subscribers are eligible to apply. Projects are listed in the *Archaeology Abroad* bulletin, published twice a year and available on subscription, price £12.50.

Contact: Archaeology Abroad, 31-34 Gordon Square, London WC1H 0PY.

Fax: 020 7383 2572.

Email: arch.abroad@ucl.ac.uk

Website: www.britarch.ac.uk/cba/archabroad

ATD Fourth World *S/W*

ATD is an international, voluntary organisation which works alongside the poorest, most disadvantaged and excluded families, in an effort to protect and guarantee their fundamental rights, including the right to family life, education and representation. Short and longer-term opportunities are offered.

The organisation recruits full-time coreworkers who can commit themselves on a long-term basis (minimum two years) to work in any of the teams in the Americas, Africa, Asia or Europe. These coreworkers support the efforts of the poor in overcoming extreme poverty and taking an active role in their community. No skills or qualifications are required as volunteers receive training in the UK first. Core workers do not choose where they will be sent, but should be available to go where ATD Fourth World feels they would be most useful.

For those interested in a short-term commitment, there is a three-month, full-time introductory programme, which takes place in London and/or Surrey. This involves manual and office work, assisting in projects with poor families, and learning about ATD Fourth World through talks, books, videos and discussions. Normally between two and five people take part and find it an enjoyable time and a great learning experience. After this programme people can decide to make a commitment of at least two years, or to join one of the teams in Europe for a shorter period.

Alternatively, workcamps are arranged in Britain and France. Here, volunteers help out with building, decorating, gardening and secretarial work and, at the same time, learn about the organisation through talks and discussions. Volunteers can also work directly with the families; activities such as street workshops and respite stays take place in Britain and Europe throughout the year. All these events last approximately two weeks.

Before they take part in any of these activities, ATD Fourth World prefers potential volunteers to attend a working weekend in London or Surrey. Applicants must be 18 years and above. No particular experience, skills or qualifications are required. However, applicants should be interested in gaining a better understanding of the causes and effects of persistent poverty, and be willing to work hard with others as part of a team. The minimum length of service is two weeks.

Volunteers on workcamps and those taking part in other activities contribute towards the cost of food and accommodation. Those who take part in the three-month introductory programme receive accommodation for the whole programme and a basic wage for the second and third months but they must contribute towards the cost of food. Those who stay longer are paid a basic salary and NI contributions.

Contact (enclosing SAE):The Director, ATD Fourth World, 48 Addington Square, London SE5 7LB.

Tel: 020 7703 3231.

Email: atd@atd.demon.co.uk

Website: www.atd-uk.org

BMS World Mission   S

BMS Action Teams enable young people aged 18 - 25 to spend time living in another country working with one of their partner churches and projects.

You would be part of a ten-month programme starting in September with one month's training in team work, crossing cultures and mission awareness, followed by six months working overseas. On returning to the UK and after more training, each four-person team spends the last two months working in churches, schools and youth groups all over Britain, talking to them about what they have been doing overseas. It is an opportunity to encourage other young people that they too have a part to play in world mission.

Each year, teams go to destinations throughout Africa, Asia, South America and the Caribbean. The work varies according to the location, but can involve youth work, children's work, evangelism, teaching, social action, using creative skills such as music and drama and supporting a local church. One team found themselves distributing aid after a cyclone hit India.

Team members are asked to raise approximately £3100 towards the cost of their overseas travel, accommodation, food, insurance, a short holiday, training and debriefing. You will be fully supported throughout by BMS staff.

BMS also run summer teams each year which run for three to five weeks throughout July and August.

Contact: Miriam Hadcocks, Mission Team Administrator, BMS World Mission, PO Box 49, Didcot, Oxon OX11 8XA.

Tel: 01235 517647. Fax: 01235 517601.

Email: actionteams@bms.org.uk

Website: www.bms.org.uk

Bouworde Flanders   W

Bouworde Flanders in Belgium organises three types of voluntary work to implement construction projects for people who need help. These are:

- workcamps during the school holidays
- projects for long-term volunteers
- projects for the Telebouworde (voluntary work in your free time).

Workcamps

These take place during the months of July, August and September. Bouworde Flanders organises workcamps (usually three weeks) in Belgium and in Austria, the Czech Republic, France, Germany, Hungary, Italy, Lithuania, Poland, Romania, Russia, the Slovak Republic, Spain, and the Ukraine. During the Christmas and Easter holidays, there are short workcamps of one week in Flanders. Volunteers of different nationalities carry out all kinds of construction work (painting, wallpapering, sanitary works, bricklaying, joinery work, electrical work). They work eight hours a day, five days a week. Technical experience and/or skills are not required; volunteers are guided and supervised by a technical leader. In exchange for their work, volunteers get free accommodation and meals. Travel costs and insurance are at the volunteer's expense.

Anyone who is 18 years and above can participate. Volunteers should be prepared to participate in every aspect of workcamp life and to respect the prevailing culture of the country they are working in. Volunteers apply by filling in an application form and paying BF1500 (approximately £24).

Long-term volunteers

Volunteers can work all year round on projects in Flanders. They carry out the same kind of work as the volunteers on workcamps. Sometimes the work is more specialised and volunteers gain more experience. Usually there are two groups of volunteers, one working near Antwerp and the other near Brussels/Leuven. Long-term volunteers are made up of all kinds of people - the unemployed, students, people taking a break from their studies or careers, and retired people. There are no special preconditions and these people work on the same conditions as those for the workcamps - 40 hours' a week work for free accommodation and meals. Applicants need to fill in an application form and pay BF1500.

Telebouworde (voluntary work in your free time)

People who want to help throughout the year but who are busy during the week can take part in Bouworde activities during the weekends. Obviously, UK citizens can only take part in the Telebouworde if they are living and working in Belgium already.

Contact: Bouworde vzw, Tiensesteenweg 157 Kessel-6, 3010 Leuven, Belgium

Tel: 00 32 16 25 91 44.

The Bridge in Britain   K/S

The Bridge in Britain scholarship programme is sponsored by the Friends of Israel Educational Trust. The scheme is designed to promote a working knowledge, and a sympathetic understanding, of the problems and achievements of the State of Israel and its peoples. Up to 12 school/college-leavers are offered a passage to Israel and free board and lodging for five creative months in Israel. Those taking part must be over 18 and in good health; no knowledge of Hebrew is required.

Under the scheme, award winners are offered a working place on a kibbutz, two months' community service in a development town, seminars and organised tours, as well as free time to travel around the country, and experience of an archaeological dig - an optional extra at the participant's expense. The back-up of specialist helpers will be available throughout the period in Israel. Places are open to all, irrespective of sex, religion or creed.

All applicants have to explain their reasons for wishing to stay in Israel in an essay (minimum of 400 words) to be submitted no later than 1 July each year. To apply, it is necessary to send a CV including date of birth, address, home telephone number, religion, academic achievements, interests and future plans, and a passport-size photo. Shortlisted candidates will be individually interviewed.

Contact: the Director, Friends of Israel Trust, PO Box 7545, London NW2 2QZ.

Fax: 020 7794 0291.

Email: foiasg@foiasg.free-online.co.uk

Camphill Village USA   S

Camphill Village is an international community of approximately 250 people, about 105 of whom are adults with learning disabilities. The village is about 100 miles north of New York city, located on 800 acres of woodland and farmland. It has a dairy farm, gardens, craft and gift shops, bakery etc, and 20 family residences in which life is shared by 5-7 adults with disabilities and 2-4 co-workers and families, often with children. Co-workers live as full-time volunteers, participating fully in village community life. Board and accommodation are provided, plus medical insurance, monthly pocket money and $600 at the end of a 12-month stay towards a three-week vacation.

Volunteers stay a minimum of six months. It is best to apply six months prior to arrival. Volunteers must pay their own air fares. Volunteers should have good social skills and, if possible, practical skills in crafts, arts, household/cooking, gardening or farming.

Contact: Camphill Village USA Inc, Copake, NY 12516, USA.
Tel: 00 1 518 329 4851. Fax: 00 1 518 329 0377.
Email: cvvolunteer@taconic.net
Website: www.camphill.org

Changing Worlds   S

Changing Worlds offer a variety of placements in a number of countries. For example, you could work as a voluntary teacher in a secondary school in Chile, Nepal or Tanzania, or you could assist in an orphanage in southern India.

Changing World looks for applicants who display initiative, determination, adaptability and social skills. Relevant experience and qualifications are welcome, although not essential. The age range is 18-35 years.

Costs vary from around £1600 to £2300 according to the placement. Prices include flights, orientation on arrival in-country, accommodation, and pre-departure briefing. Departure dates are September, January and March. Apply as early as you can.

There are also paid opportunities (described in chapter 9).

Contact: Changing Worlds, 11 Doctors Lane, Chaldon, Surrey CR3 5AE.
Tel: 01883 340960. Fax: 01883 330783.
Email: careers@changingworlds.co.uk
Website: www.changingworlds.co.uk

Profile   Lucy Western

Primary school teaching in Tanzania with Changing Worlds

'During my second year at college I decided that, rather than going straight to university after completing my A levels, I would defer my place for a year and undertake one of the many different gap year projects I had heard about.

I decided to take a year out for a variety of reasons. I didn't feel ready to continue with my education. I wanted to see some of the world and experience a very different way of life, which I hoped would make me more focused when I began university. I was also very interested in teaching, and I thought spending six months in the job would help me decide whether or not it was the career for me.

My college was very helpful, and gave me a number of different contact addresses, all related to different volunteer projects, or jobs abroad.

In the end I chose a placement based in Tanzania working as a primary school teacher with a company called Changing Worlds. Once I was accepted for this placement, I set about raising the funds to get there. This was very tiring and took a long time, but, in the end it was incredibly rewarding knowing I'd got there through my own hard work.

In total I spent eight months in Tanzania - six months teaching and two months travelling. The whole trip was a fantastic experience. It opened my eyes to very different cultures and lifestyles, and I learnt a great deal about the people and the country. I developed vocational skills such as teaching. I also learnt how to cope without parents always around.

I did have some doubts about the placement, particularly prior to my departure. I had no idea what to expect once I arrived in Tanzania, and it was the first time I was going to be completely independent. However, once I arrived, there were so many new experiences that I didn't once regret my decision. I enjoyed every moment and relished each new experience, such as teaching a class of 50 eager ten-year olds, or being taught playground games in Swahili. I went on school outings to local safari parks where we saw lions, elephants, monkeys and other animals I had never dreamt of seeing in the wild. Even shopping for my daily groceries wasn't a chore but an exercise in trying to barter for fruit and veg in another language.

Overall the trip was a fantastic experience. I made lifelong friends with many of the teachers and pupils and visited some amazing places. I learnt more living in Tanzania for eight months than I ever imagined possible.'

Profile   **Peter Hill**

To India with Changing Worlds

'I had graduated from university like many of my friends, with a degree, but little idea what to do with it. After a year spent in an office watching rain stream down the windows, I knew that I wanted to see a bit of the world, but didn't fancy just lying on a beach for six months.

I had always harboured a faint interest in teaching, so when I heard that Changing Worlds were looking for volunteers to begin a programme of English teaching with a non-governmental organisation in India, I applied.

Within a few months I found myself working on an Indian rural development project – The People's Craft Training Centre. This was

133

the focal point for the local community, for example, working alongside local farmers on water-efficient farming techniques, advising young women on healthcare, and visiting teachers in local schools, checking on the integration of children with physical and learning difficulties. Through one of its other schemes, I taught spoken English in a local high school, and although I had no teaching experience, and hardly any Tamil, the enthusiasm of the students gave me the confidence to try more involved lessons.

Using what little facilities the school had available, the students presented talks on the school's herb garden, wrote reports on inter-schools hockey matches and 'brought' things in to stock up 'Sir's shop'. There's nothing like being thrown in at the deep end to get your creative juices flowing!

The solitude of life in rural India was counterbalanced by the friendliness I encountered everywhere, and the generosity found in even the poorest homes. I was fortunate to live among Indian friends, and was invited to eat in their homes, watch their televisions (surely the worst TV in the world) and even play for their village cricket teams! Working alongside Indian people, I felt as if I had seen aspects of the country from a closer perspective than I did when travelling around in the final weeks of my stay.

The difficulties I encountered certainly gave me a different perspective. Having an unbroken supply of electricity and water on the same day is a rarity in India, so finding adverts for slimming products on British TV when I returned provided almost as much of a culture shock as that which I experienced on my first day in Madras.

I am currently looking for a job with a charity or something in development work.'

Chantiers de Jeunes, Provence Côte d'Azur   **W**

This organisation offers voluntary work opportunities for those aged 14-17 years. Volunteers work five hours per day, six days per week for one week during the school year, or two weeks in the summer. There are places for 14 volunteers (seven female, seven male). The work involves environmental protection, and volunteers work on a 17th-century fort on the Isle Ste Marguerite (Cannes). Young people meet others of different nationalities and are responsible for doing their own food shopping, and preparing and cooking meals. There are watersports, games and shows in the afternoons and evenings. Volunteers pay their own travel and FF2100 (approx £210) for membership, food, accommodation, work, activities and insurance.

Contact: Chantiers de Jeunes Provence Côte d'Azur, Maison des Chantiers-Ferme Giaume, 7 Avenue Pierre de Coubertin, 06150 Cannes-

La Bocca, France.
Tel: 00 33 04 93 47 89 69. Fax: 00 33 04 93 48 12 01.
Email: cjpca@club-internet.fr
Website: www.club-internet.fr/perso/cjpca

Church Mission Society (CMS)   S

CMS can help young Christians in the 18-30 age range to gain experience of a different culture through *ENCOUNTER*. Summer visits are arranged to Africa, Asia and Eastern Europe, and they provide an opportunity for young people to live alongside Christians from another culture, sharing their lifestyle, witness, worship, hopes and aspirations.

Each group usually consists of up to ten participants, with two experienced leaders who encourage the group to share and reflect together. The emphasis is put on the experience to be gained and not on the work contribution, although work projects are often part of the experience, e.g. tree planting, decorating a hospital.

CMS also provides opportunities for people to gain experience of the church in a different culture through its *Make a Difference* programme, either overseas or in the UK. This means that participants will be either working in the UK or alongside their partner churches in Asia, the Middle East, Eastern Europe and in some African countries. The aim of the programme is not so much about giving as receiving and gaining cross-cultural experience, while learning something about the church in another environment and having an opportunity to develop one's own personal faith in the light of these new experiences. By going on such a programme, young people may be better equipped to play a part in a world mission.

Participants need to be 21-30 at the start of the *Make a Difference* placement and between 18 and 30 at the start of a Britain Placement. The length of placements varies between six and eighteen months. For visa purposes, a degree or professional qualification may be required to work in some countries, as well as having a real and living faith and the willingness to learn from other cultures, and to share the experience with one's church and community on returning home.

CMS provides the cost of training but participants are responsible for other costs. The total cost of an overseas placement is approximately £2000.

Contact: Experience Programmes Adviser, Partnership House, CMS, 157 Waterloo Road, London SE1 8UU.
Tel: 020 7928 8681. Fax: 020 7401 3215.
Email: kathy.tyson@cms-uk.org
Website: www.cms-uk.org

Concordia W

Concordia is a non-profit-making charity. It works in conjunction with international voluntary youth organisations which organise international workcamps worldwide. Projects last two or three weeks, from the end of June until mid-September. In addition work can be arranged on farms in Norway (for up to three months) and in the French- and German-speaking cantons of Switzerland (for up to two months between March and November). Pocket money is paid in these cases.

Accommodation and conditions vary considerably, from youth hostels to tents. Volunteers must be prepared to cope with simple, often basic, conditions.

The nature of the work varies; many projects are concerned with nature conservation and environmental protection. Others provide work on the restoration of monuments and castles, construction, community and social work, counselling on children's camps and some English language teaching. As a rule, volunteers work a five- or five-and-a-half-day week, though hours can vary. Participating in a workcamp challenges a volunteer's skills, inner resources and initiative and can also be excellent fun.

A registration fee is charged, but this varies from country to country; usually ranging between £75 and £100. The fee covers board and lodging and, in most cases, insurance against accidents while at the camp. Sports, social activities and excursions are often arranged during free time. Volunteers pay their own travel costs, and are responsible for travel arrangements, visas, etc.

Applicants must be between 16 and 30 years old. In some cases, the upper age limit is 26. As the work is strenuous, physical fitness is essential. Volunteers are expected to participate in all aspects of camp life. A working knowledge of a foreign language may be required, but is not always essential. English is used as the language of communication at most camps. For many projects, previous voluntary workcamp experience is not required.

Contact (enclosing SAE): International Volunteer Co-ordinator, Concordia, 20-22 Heversham House, Boundary Road, Hove BN3 4ET.
Tel: 01273 422218. Fax: 01273 421182.
Email: info@concordia-iye.org.uk
Website: www.concordia-iye.org.uk

Conservation Volunteers Australia (CVA) C

Conservation Volunteers Australia is a national not-for-profit, community organisation founded in 1982. CVA completes in excess of 1,500 conservation projects Australia-wide each year, and welcomes both Australian and international volunteers. For A$23 per night,

CVA provides food, project-related transport and accommodation, which may vary according to the location of the project. Volunteers work in teams of six to ten under the guidance of a CVA team leader who coordinates the project and provides training as required.

A CVA volunteer experience offers the opportunity to contribute in a practical way to the conservation of Australia's environment. Projects undertaken by CVA include tree planting, erosion and salinity control, seed collection, construction and maintenance of walking tracks, flora and fauna surveys, weed control, revegetation and heritage site restoration.

CVA has offices Australia wide, and volunteers may nominate any Friday throughout the year as a preferred starting date.

Contact: Conservation Volunteers Australia, PO Box 423, Ballarat, Victoria 3353.

Tel: 00 61 5333 1483. Fax: 00 61 5333 2166.

Email: info@conservationvolunteers.com.au

Website: www.conservationvolunteers.com.au

Coral Cay Conservation   C

This organisation offers the opportunity to join a team of international volunteers aged 16+, working with an established, award-winning, not-for-profit conservation group. You can help local communities protect fragile coral reef systems, or fast disappearing rainforest – or do both. Since 1986, hundreds of volunteers have joined each year. With their support, the organisation has helped to establish eight marine and wildlife reserves, including the new Belize Barrier Reef World Heritage Site. Coral Cay Conservation currently has expeditions in Fiji, Honduras and the Philippines. Expeditions are for a minimum of three weeks, and run throughout the year. No experience is necessary, as full training is provided.

Contact: Coral Cay Conservation Ltd, The Tower, 13th Floor, 125 High Street, Colliers Wood, London SW19 2JG.

Tel: 0870 750 0668. Fax: 0870 750 0667.

Email: info@coralcay.org

Website: www.coralcay.org

Cotravaux   W

Cotravaux is a co-ordinating organisation of 12 French and international associations, providing general information about them and promoting their voluntary work. They offer camps in France lasting for two or three weeks, revolving around social or manual work (renovation, construction, land-clearing, nature preservation, restoration of ancient monuments, archaeological digs, etc). The minimum age for volunteers on most camps is 18. However, some accept volunteers younger than this; a very few accept volunteers as young as 14.

Contact: Cotravaux at 11 rue de Clichy, 75009 Paris, France.

Tel: 00 33 1 48 74 7920. Fax: 00 33 1 48 74 7401.

Email: cotravaux@aol.com

Earthwatch   C

Founded in the USA 28 years ago, Earthwatch opened its European office in Oxford in 1985. A non-profit-making organisation, Earthwatch's aim is to match field scientists needing money and personnel with members of the public willing to help. Its services are in great demand since scientific funding is drying up at a time when ecological problems are multiplying.

Earthwatch serves as a bridge between the public and the scientific community. To date, Earthwatch has co-ordinated the involvement of thousands of men and women in research expeditions worldwide. It has contributed over £22.5 million and over 4,450,000 hours of labour to earth, human and life sciences in the field. Over 2,000 scientists in 150 countries have been assisted by Earthwatch team members over the past 28 years.

Earthwatch team members share the costs of mobilising the research expeditions. For two or three weeks, team members may learn to excavate, map, photograph, gather data, make collections, assist diving operations and share all other field chores associated with professional expedition research. No special skills are required.

Once in the field, volunteers' contributions, which vary with the nature of the project but which currently average £900, cover all the costs, excluding travel. Students and teachers may apply for Earthwatch fellowship grants. Accommodation can range from tents to hotels, and meals are usually local dishes. Earthwatch publishes an annual catalogue, containing information on all its projects worldwide. Membership is also available at £25 per annum or £15 for students.

Contact: Earthwatch Europe, 57 Woodstock Road, Oxford OX2 6HJ.

Tel: 01865 318838. Fax: 01865 311383.

Email: info@earthwatch.org.uk

Website: www.earthwatch.org.uk/europe

EIL – Community Service   C/S

EIL has opportunities in for voluntary work for individual participants in a number of different countries, including: Argentina and Ecuador (for a minimum of three months including one month language support) and Thailand (for a minimum of five weeks). Costs vary according to the programme. Language tuition is included. EIL also arranges gap year opportunities for groups – ranging from four weeks environmental work in Canada to two to three weeks in Costa Rica, undertaking environmental and community work.

Contact: EIL, 287 Worcester Road, Malvern, Worcs, WR14 1AB.

Tel: 01684 562577. Fax: 01684 562212.

Email: info@eiluk.org

Website: www.eiluk.org

Emmaus International   W

Emmaus is an international movement made up of 350 communities and groups in 37 countries throughout the world. It aims at sharing with those living in moral and material misery, and fighting on both public and private levels against the causes of such destitution. The movement was originally set up in France but now operates throughout the world.

Emmaus International organises workcamps in Europe for 15 days a month or more. The camps are for people aged 18 and above who want to have a practical experience of sharing. The work involves reprocessing used objects (clothes, scrap and furniture), sorting, repairing and selling these items. Board and accommodation are usually provided.

Contact: Emmaus International, 183 bis rue Vaillant Couturrier, BP 91, F-94143 Alfortville, Cedex.

Tel: 00 33 1 4893 2950.

Email: contact@emmaus-international.org

Website: www.emmaus-international.org

European Voluntary Service (EVS)   C/S

EVS is for 18 to 25-year-olds who can spend six to 12 months working in another European country. A wide range of voluntary placements are available. All expenses are paid – food, accommodation, pocket money, international travel and medical insurance. Places are competitive. It is best to plan a minimum of nine months ahead.

Contact: EVS Office, EIL, 287 Worcester Road, Malvern, Worcester WR14 1AB.

Tel: 01684 562577. Fax: 01684 562212.

Email: info@eiluk.org

Website: www.eiluk.org

Frontier   *C*

Frontier is a non-profit-making organisation that brings together the conservation needs of developing countries with the commitment and enthusiasm of volunteers from around the world. At a time when ecological crises are multiplying and the resources to deal with them are diminishing, the Frontier initiative brings people aged 17 and over, untrained in conservation techniques, to the forefront of conservation research, enabling them to become involved in vital scientific work in the field.

Since Frontier's inception in 1989, well over 450,000 hours of research have been undertaken by volunteers in areas under threat in Madagascar, Mozambique, Tanzania, Uganda and Vietnam. Currently working alongside scientists and conservation organisations in Madagascar, Tanzania and Vietnam, each Frontier project represents a unique and valuable scientific investigation. Volunteers, who come from many backgrounds, spend ten weeks implementing a research programme that draws on their strengths as an expeditionary team. Unlike other organisations, the initiative comes from the volunteers themselves - a quality that is looked for when Frontier recruits volunteers.

If selected, volunteers are encouraged to participate in every part of the project, from data collection and surveys to fetching supplies from the local village. The 'hands-on' experience is such that many Frontier volunteers subsequently move on to work in conservation fields.

Each Frontier project is self-funded with the expeditionary team contributing to the cost of the expedition. Frontier volunteers are expected to raise around £2500 for ten weeks and around £3800 for twenty weeks (excluding flights and visa costs). Comprehensive advice on fundraising is made available to all potential volunteers. Frontier arranges visas/work permits which enable volunteers to travel around the country they visit after the expedition.

Contact: Frontier, 50-52 Rovington Street. London EC2A 3QP.

Tel: 020 7613 2422. Fax: 020 7613 2992.

Email: enquiries@frontier.ac.uk

Website: www.frontier.ac.uk

GAP Activity Projects (GAP) Ltd   *C/S*

GAP is an educational charity which each year organises voluntary work opportunities for over 1400 British 18-19 year olds during their year out between school/college and higher education, training or employment. Projects are available in over 30 countries around the world. They typically last from four to nine months and include assisting with the teaching of English, helping with general activities in schools, care work and hospital projects, participating in practical conservation work and working on outdoor education camps.

The volunteer must meet his or her own travel and insurance costs, as well as a GAP fee of £515, which covers general administration of the projects and the costs of GAP's unpaid volunteer staff who set up and run the projects. If teaching English as a foreign language, a short TEFL course (approximately £200) may also be required. During the placement food, accommodation and in many cases pocket money are provided.

The GAP brochure is available from August onwards each year for placements starting a year later. Students should apply at any time, but the earlier the better. Every applicant is offered an interview and these take place in Reading, Leeds, Glasgow and Dublin. A number of regional interviews are also held. All candidates must be 18 at the start of their placement.

Contact: GAP Activity Projects (GAP) Ltd, 44 Queen's Road, Reading RG1 4BB.

Tel: 0118 9594914. Fax: 0118 9576634.

Email: volunteer@gap.org.uk

Website: www.gap.org.uk

Profile Jessica Crellin
To South Africa with GAP

'My sister had taken a year out with GAP in Mexico and had such an amazing time that I decided that I too wanted an opportunity to see the world from a different perspective, and sample a way of living that was far removed from the one I was used to. The reason I chose South Africa was that I was curious to see a country for which individuals like Mandela had sacrificed so much, and also to see the reality of the 'Rainbow Nation' in the new post-apartheid era.

My project was for six months in a school for children with cerebral palsy in a township of Cape Town. Initially I was fairly apprehensive of the school as I had no previous experience of looking after disabled children, and most of the school's first language was Afrikaans which I didn't understand at all. However the staff were incredibly welcoming and made us feel part of the team, and it wasn't too long before we were picking up some Afrikaans, though I would hardly say I was totally fluent!

I worked largely within the occupational and speech therapy departments of the school, which was eye-opening; my learning curve on cerebral palsy in the first weeks was almost vertical!! I was given *my own English-speaking groups and individuals to work with, which was initially a little strange as I had only ever been the pupil. I found it immensely rewarding, especially when the children learned something new and could remember it for the next class!! Most memorable was the children's determination to enjoy life despite their disabilities - their smiling faces are some of the most vivid images I have.*

Looking back now I remember my time abroad in a series of memories - the sound of wheelchairs, crutches and feet going to breakfast every morning, sunset on Table Mountain, barbecues on the beach with friends, travelling round southern Africa in my vacation, the sadness of having to leave the best time of my life - so far!

What have I gained? I have to say that all the clichés are true; I learned not only independence but self reliance and a knowledge that I can handle myself in very varied situations. Armed with these 'new' qualities I feel I have approached university with a better sense of perspective. The legacy of the year in Cape Town is that having glimpsed a little of the world I am now desperate to see more.'

Profile **Mark Lancaster**

Grape picking in France and to Malaysia with GAP

'A levels are over and it is decision time. I, like many others, chose a year out which is one of the best decisions I have ever made. I wanted a challenge, a chance to see another part of the world, a different culture and to have a break from education.

September came and I set off with two other friends to France to raise money grape picking. Four weeks later with shredded hands, a car full of wine and aching backs we had seen it through to the end and had learnt a great deal. In future I could really appreciate a bottle of wine, having learnt how the grape finally reaches the table.

On my return to England I set about getting a job to prepare myself for my trip to Malaysia with the GAP organisation.

Next thing I knew I was touching down in Kuala Lumpur with £1500 in the bank, ready to teach English and woodwork. Everyone was so welcoming and friendly and once I had begun to settle in, get used to the heat, three showers a day, the teaching awaited. Progress was slow but extremely rewarding. Of course there were times when I got sick of it, but I worked through it and it made me a stronger character. The wonderful thing is you don't have to live out of a rucksack for eight months. I had a base, which enabled me to make local friends and see Malaysia bit by bit. Soaking up the sun on the tropical beaches, enjoying the exotic fruits and water-sports, visiting the many temples, museums and wonderful markets. Malaysia is a country made up of Malays, Chinese and Indians, each contributing a different religion and cuisine.

My stopover in Thailand for two weeks enabled me to see another country and enjoy a trek. Upon my reluctant return home, my college place awaited.

In my view it is important to secure the place you want before you set off. It is also important, if a gap year is for you, to plan carefully. Too many of my friends have just wasted their year with little to show. A constructive year helping others, makes you a far better person, broadens your perspective on life and prepares you for later life, which comes upon us too soon. In my view it also helps secure a job in later life. Only take a one-year break, two will make it impossible to settle back into education. Take the challenge while you have the opportunity.'

Global Vision International   C

GVI expeditions offer the adventurous individual the chance to work as part of a team, alongside host country organisations, gaining skills in conservation, leadership and teamwork. Examples of opportunities (which range from three weeks to one year) include: five weeks tracking elephants in the African bush; three months scuba diving in the Caribbean; one year working in Alaska. No experience is necessary, as full training is given. Applicants must be aged 18+. Apply six months before you are available. Costs are from £500.

Contact: Global Vision International, Amwell Farm House, Nomansland, Wheathampstead, St Albans, Herts AL4 8EJ.

Tel: 01582 831300. Fax: 01582 831302.

Email: GVIenquiries@aol.com

Website: www.gvi.co.uk

Greenforce   C

Greenforce is a registered non-profit-making organisation, which arranges environmental conservation expeditions overseas, mostly in developing countries, which do not have the resources or personnel to conduct the necessary research and development themselves. Projects, which include biodiversity surveys in Uganda and Zambia and a coral reef survey in Fiji, Borneo and the Bahamas, are led by qualified scientists and experienced camp leaders. They work closely with the host country government departments and universities, and the work is often related to the development of a wildlife reserve or ecotourism development. Volunteers join the project for ten weeks, leaving in January, April, July or October each year. Many volunteers use the time as valuable fieldwork experience before seeking a career in environmental conservation, and there are some opportunities for paid employment with, or postgraduate funding by Greenforce, after a period as a volunteer.

Volunteers must be over 18, committed, enthusiastic and adventurous. They need to raise £2550, which includes training in the UK and the host country, an information pack, a medical pack, food, accommodation, visas and insurance. Greenforce also provides a pack full of information and ideas about how to raise this sum of money. Monthly open evenings are arranged where potential volunteers can discuss the options and choose which project to apply for.

Contact: Greenforce, 11-15 Betterton Street, Covent Garden, London WC2H 9BP.

Tel: 020 7470 8888. Fax: 020 7470 8889.

Email: greenforce@btinternet.com

Website: www.greenforce.org

Gruppo Volontari Della Svizzera Italiana (GVSI)   W

The GVSI is a group consisting of adults and young people in the Italian part of Switzerland who welcome foreigners who want to take part in an international workcamp. At present, there are about 100 active members of the group. Volunteers must be 18 and above. Volunteers are involved in reconstruction and maintenance work after natural disasters and they are involved in helping the aged by, for example, cutting wood, helping in their homes, in stables, in orchards, etc. Group members allocate other work such as cooking, cleaning and shopping between them. Volunteers are given a house in the village to live in. Camps last from 1 June to 30 September and volunteers usually stay for one or two weeks.

Contact: Gruppo Volontari Della Svizzera Italiana (GVSI), C.P 12, 6517 Arbedo, Switzerland.

Tel: 00 41 91 857 4520. Fax: 00 41 91 682 9272.

i-to-i   C/S

Operates i.Venture voluntary projects. Volunteers work on English teaching, conservation and work projects in Sri Lanka, India, Nepal, Thailand, China, Mongolia, Ghana, Uganda, Bolivia, Costa Rica, Ecuador, Australia and Russia. Placements are flexible and last for two weeks to twelve months. TEFL (teaching English as a foreign language) training is provided in the UK before departure. The programme includes full country orientation, field staff, board and lodging.

i.Venture is open to those aged 18 upwards. Costs for three months are £750 plus airfare.

Inspired, a free quarterly news magazine featuring travel and work ideas, is available from i-to-i.

Contact: i-to-i, 9 Blenheim Terrace, Leeds LS2 9HZ.

Tel: 0870 333 2332. Fax: 0113 274 6923.

Email: travel@i-to-i.com

Website: www.i-to-i.com

Indian Volunteers for Community Service   S

Learn about rural life and development work by spending between three weeks and six months on a rural development project in Uttar Pradesh. Applicants need to be over 18, able to travel independently and to be flexible and patient! Volunteers pay all their own costs and receive no remuneration.

Apply four to six months in advance. The scheme runs between September and March each year.

Contact: Indian Volunteers for Community Service, 12 Eastleigh Avenue, Harrow HA2 0UF.

Tel: 020 8864 4740. Fax: 020 8930 8338.

Email: enquiries@ives.org.uk

Website: www.ives.org.uk

Insight Nepal   S

Insight Nepal believes that serving others is one of the most worthwhile of human endeavours. The main objective of this programme is to provide opportunities to those who are interested in gaining a cultural experience by contributing their time and skills to benefit community service groups throughout Nepal. The second objective is to help those who are looking for an opportunity to reach people and community groups who are in need of their skills.

Volunteers spend from one to three months on the programme. Applicants must be aged 18-65, and have achieved an A level standard education. Teaching, working or volunteering experience is desirable but not necessary. Prospective volunteers should be flexible, fit and willing to immerse themselves in another culture. Volunteers are welcomed with skills of all types and from all backgrounds. The costs are a US$40 application fee, and US$400-800 programme fee.

Contact: Insight Nepal, PO Box 489, Zero K.M., Pokhara, Kaski, Nepal.
Tel: 00 977 61 30266
Email: insight@mos.com.np
Website: www.south-asia.com/insight

International Voluntary Service (IVS)   W

IVS is a voluntary organisation that exists to provide opportunities for voluntary work for people, both in the UK and overseas, in the belief that this will further international understanding and lead to a more just and peaceful world.

IVS recruits volunteers who are over 18, to work in about 50 workcamps in Britain and hundreds more in over 30 countries abroad, including Eastern and Western Europe, North Africa and the USA. The length of a workcamp ranges from two to four weeks. The work carried out varies enormously and can include any of the following:

- campaigning on issues related to developing countries, racism, disarmament and peace education
- working with people with disabilities, children or the elderly, either in their own homes, at a day centre or on a holiday
- ecological and environmental work
- women's camps
- artistic/cultural camps.

The workcamp group will normally be made up of between six and twenty volunteers from at least three/four different countries. The volunteers live and work together, sharing responsibility for the organisation of the work and domestic arrangements, such as cooking and cleaning. In return for the work they carry out, volunteers receive basic food and accommodation free. Most workcamps take place between June and September but there are others running at different times of the year. Early application is advised.

Workcamps help to support communities by providing outside assistance to projects undertaking worthwhile voluntary work. At the same time, they offer opportunities for volunteers to meet new people, learn skills and have some fun. Living together in an international group, volunteers learn about different lifestyles and cultures. The experience of living in a community frequently has a marked impact on people and influences the rest of their lives.

For more information, contact one of the IVS UK offices listed below.

IVS North, *Castle Hill House, 21 Otley Road, Headingley, Leeds LS6 3AA.*
Tel: 0113 230 4600.

IVS Scotland, 7 *Upper Bow, Edinburgh EH1 2JN.*
Tel: 0131 226 6722.

IVS South, Old Hall, East Bergholt, Colchester, Essex CO7 6TQ.
Tel: 01206 298215.

Involvement Volunteers Association Inc   *C/S*

Involvement Volunteers Association Inc (IVI) aims to assist people to travel worldwide and be involved in volunteer activities which may be either related to the care and sustainable development of the natural environment, or the care of and assistance for disadvantaged people through social service activities in foreign countries.

Networked International Volunteering provides opportunities for young people to travel and take part, even though they may have little or no experience but are genuinely interested to try themselves out by volunteering before gaining further education. Others are seeking to gain some experience after finishing their course.

Placements generally run for a minimum of two weeks, except the social service placements which run for a minimum of six weeks as the hosts or 'clients' need time to gain confidence in the volunteer.

Placements are available in Australia, Argentina, China, Ecuador, Germany, Fiji, India, Nepal, New Zealand, Sabah (Malaysia), Thailand, Samoa, South Africa, the United Kingdom, Venezuela and other countries in Asia, the Americas, Europe or the Pacific region, through IVI and the network of IVAssociates.

In 2001/2002, the costs include a registration fee (about £80), which is not refundable but is not payable again for any subsequent trips in life; a multiple placement programme fee for a programme with any number of placements in any number of countries over a maximum of 12 months (about £145) or a single placement fee with just one placement in one country (about £95). Each placement has a minimum placement fee (about £30) which can include accommodation and food. The placement fee becomes the cancellation fee if necessary. In some countries the organisations are not able to provide more than accommodation, but food is then quite cheap.

After making application to IVI, the volunteer (or pairs of volunteers) then receives a suggested programme as requested, which can be changed until it suits the volunteer to accept it, by payment of the confirmation fee. The programme can include special events of interest to volunteers and coach passes at discounted rates, as well as advice about travel.

Contact: Involvement Volunteers Association Inc, PO Box 218, Port Melbourne, Victoria 3207, Australia.
Tel: 00 61 3 9646 9392. Fax: 00 61 3 9646 5504.

Email: ivworldwide@volunteering.org.au
Website: www.volunteering.org.au

Contact: Involvement Volunteers – United Kingdom, 7 Bushmead Ave, Kingskerswell, Newton Abbot, Devon TQ12 5EN.

Tel: 01803 872 594.
Email: ivengland@volunteering.org.au

Jacob's Well Appeal   S (EXP)

A registered charity offering voluntary work for between four weeks and three months in a neuropsychiatric hospital in Northern Romania providing contact and human stimulation to child patients, largely through play activities. Volunteers also help at a day centre for children with disabilities who are living at home.

Minimum age is 18. Older applicants with relevant professional qualifications - such as physiotherapists, special needs teachers and nurses - are particularly welcome. Volunteers pay their own expenses. Apply at least six months in advance.

Contact: Jacob's Well Appeal, 2 Ladygate, Beverley, East Yorkshire HU17 8BH.
Tel: 01482 881162. Fax: 01482 865452.
Email: thejacobswell@aol.com

Kibbutz Representatives   K

Kibbutz Representatives runs a number of schemes including the popular Working Visitor Scheme, and limited places on the Working Hebrew Scheme, which enables the participant to experience kibbutz life while providing the time to learn conversational Hebrew. The organisation can also arrange participation on desert treks, diving courses and nature trails, at the end of the kibbutz period, for an additional cost.

The Working Visitor Scheme

To apply, you need to be between 18 and 32 and be in good physical and mental health. You must be able to commit yourself for at least eight weeks. You will be expected to work hard, six to eight hours a day, six days a week, at whatever is assigned to you, be it agricultural or industrial work, or in one of the services (i.e. dining room, laundry, clothes store, kitchen). You will be living two to four to a room, and the conditions could be fairly basic. You will be expected to conform to the regulations of the kibbutz while you are there. All applicants are interviewed.

In return for your commitment and hard work, you will receive food and lodging, laundry services, a small allowance and the recreational and other facilities that the kibbutz has to offer. There will also be the possibility of organised trips to places of interest. You will have the opportunity to experience an alternative lifestyle.

It is essential to apply early as the scheme is popular. The application process can take between three and five weeks or longer in busy periods. Places for the summer are in high demand. Usually the minimum length of time you can spend on a kibbutz is eight weeks and the maximum is usually three months. Any application to extend the stay needs to be made in Israel. The cost of this scheme is £45 registration, plus flight and insurance.

Contact: Kibbutz Representatives, 1a Accommodation Road, London NW11 8ED.
Tel: 020 8458 9235. Fax: 020 8455 7930.
Email: enquiries@kibbutz.org.uk

The Mission to Seafarers   S

The Mission to Seafarers organises voluntary opportunities in the shipping industry for young Christian men and women. Volunteers are based in 18 ports around the world in Europe, the Far East and Africa. Volunteers assist a port chaplain and work may involve visiting ships, practical work such as gardening, visiting hospitals, conducting sight-seeing tours, arranging sporting events, helping with worship, serving in the seafarers' centre's bar and shop, etc.

Applicants must be at least 21 and hold a valid driving licence. They should be Anglican or a member of another Christian denomination and be prepared to participate fully in Anglican ministry and worship. The average length of service is one year, and 18 volunteers are recruited each year. Free board and accommodation are provided and travel fares are paid.

Applications should ideally be made by the end of March to start July/August/September the same year.

Contact: the Ministry Secretary, The Mission to Seafarers, St Michael Paternoster Royal, College Hill, London EC4R 2RL.
Tel: 020 7248 5202. Fax: 020 7248 4761.
Email: ministry@missiontoseafarers.org

National Youth Council of Ireland

For information on voluntary work in the Republic of Ireland contact:

Information Officer, National Youth Council of Ireland, 3 Montague Street, Dublin 2.
Tel: 00 353 1478 4122. Fax: 00 353 1478 3974.
Email: info@nyci.ie
Website: www.youth.ie

Operation Mobilisation S

Operation Mobilisation is an international, interdenominational evangelical Christian mission agency which has more than 2800 people serving in evangelism, establishing new churches, and community development in more than 60 countries. Service with OM can vary from short-term (1-4 weeks) teams in the summer to lifelong career mission work. Gap year students can join for between six and 12 months, either in August or January, and work in countries in Western Europe, the Middle East, South Asia, South Africa or on one of our ships, which visit ports around the world with their 'floating bookshops'. Life on an Operation Mobilisation team will provide a blend of training in evangelism and Christian discipleship, with experience of living in a different culture or in an international community. Team members may be working in various types of evangelistic work, often in cooperation with local churches, or using their practical or administrative skills on one of our ships or in support base.

Contact: Personnel Department, Operation Mobilisation, The Quinta, Weston Rhyn, Oswestry, Shropshire SY10 7LT.

Tel: 01691 773388. Fax: 01691 778378.

Email: join.us@uk.om.org

Website: www.uk.om.org

pro international e.V W

This German organisation offers unpaid voluntary work in international workcamps. Camp work can involve organising children's holidays, environmental work, renovation, etc. Volunteers usually stay two to three weeks and insurance, board and accommodation are free.

Contact: pro international e.V, Bahnhofstrasse 26A, 35037 Marburg, Germany.

Tel: 00 49 6421 65277. Fax: 00 49 6421 64407.

Email: pro-international@lahn.net

Website: www.pro-international.de

Project Trust C/S

Project Trust is an educational charity with 33 years of experience in organising years abroad for 17 to 19-year-olds. Their selection, training and debriefing courses aim to ensure that participants get the most out of their time. Participants may spend a full year overseas. They can learn the language and live as a member of the local community. During their holidays, participants have the opportunity to travel and explore.

Project Trust has a range of projects in 24 countries throughout Central and South America, Africa, Asia and the Middle East. Examples of projects include: spending a year running a newspaper in Namibia; teaching English at a university in Cuba; being a sailing and climbing assistant at an Outward Bound School in Hong Kong, Malaysia or Sri Lanka; working at a children's home project; teaching at a primary school; helping with desert conservation in Morocco.

Contact: Project Trust, The Hebridean Centre, Isle of Coll, Argyll PA78 6TE.

Tel: 01879 230444. Fax: 01879 230 357.

Email: info@projecttrust.org.uk

Website: www.projecttrust.org.uk

Profile Nancy MacDonald
To Thailand with Project Trust

'When I was in the Lower Sixth we had a speaker who had been overseas with an organisation called Project Trust in her gap year. I decided there and then this was the organisation for me.

My Upper Sixth year was spent in a whirl of excitement and terror. On the one hand I had A levels to take, endless revision, and then the actual exams themselves.

I applied to Project Trust, and spent an amazing week in the Hebrides, where they have their headquarters, on one of their selection courses. Many of the staff had done Project Trust themselves, so it was fun talking to them about their experiences. I enjoyed that week and it was great to hear that I was going to go to Thailand, the land of my dreams.

My parents and I attended a fund raising workshop in the winter. It was good to get together with others in my area to find out what they were doing to raise the funds. We decided to run a joint disco, which raised £1000 in the end, but split five ways it was not a great deal each. So we decided to run events individually after that. By the time I reached my A levels I had raised my target figure of just over £3000 and I was really, really proud of myself. I felt I had achieved something important and it gave me even more determination to go overseas and make a success of my year.

I was teaching in a large government school in Kamphang Phet, with my partner Katie. We took classes between us, of perhaps fifty children. We were told to get the children to speak English, and at first it seemed an impossible task because they were so shy. They would sit looking at us whilst Katie and I tried jumping around like clowns to *make them speak. This went on for some weeks until one day we had an inspiration. We ran a competition for them in which they could not participate unless they spoke English. It was amazing how much English they remembered when they discovered they could not win without speaking English. From then on Katie and I never looked back.*

During our holidays we went all round the country. Project Trust laid on a Thai language course during our first holidays which was very useful. But in the end I could speak the language quite well.

I cannot say we did not have moments when we missed our home and family, and when my dog died at home I was miserable for weeks. We had a representative in Bangkok who was brilliant. She heard I was upset and invited me and Katie to spend the weekend with her and her husband.

It was devastating to say goodbye to all our friends. The teachers cried, and so did we. Our students presented us with two pictures, which we managed to get back home without breaking.

I am now at university. The first term was difficult and I really missed Thailand. By the second term I had more or less come to terms with the fact that my life had moved on and that university could also be fun. But whatever else happens in my life I can honestly say that my year in Thailand with Project Trust is going to remain the most unforgettable and formative of my life.'

Projects Abroad   C/S

Linked to Teaching Abroad (see later in this chapter), but provides medical, conservation, business and other unpaid work experience placements to suit various levels of ability, qualification and experience. Volunteers pay their own expenses.

Contact: Projects Abroad, Gerrard House, Rustington, West Sussex BN16 1AW.

Tel: 01903 859911. Fax: 01903 785779

Email: info@teaching-abroad.co.uk

Website: www.teaching-abroad.co.uk

Quaker Voluntary Action (QVA)   C/S/W

QVA provides placements for volunteers from many backgrounds. Placements are short-term (usually 2-4 weeks – where you work with a group of volunteers, but longer projects, where you are placed individually, are under development). The placement programme builds on existing links with schemes supported by Quaker International Social Projects. There is a wide variety of placements available, ranging from community arts work in Belfast, park-building in Russia to organic farm work in Italy. The summer programme is

published in Spring. A registration fee is charged and travel costs are paid by the volunteer. Basic accommodation and food are provided.
Contact: QVA, 6 Mount Street, Manchester M2 5NS.
Email: mail@qva.org.uk
Website:qva.org.uk

Quest Overseas   C/S

Offers volunteers three-month expeditions to South America and Africa. South American projects begin with a three-week Spanish course in Quito, Ecuador, followed by a month working on a community project, such as looking after children in Peru, or on a conservation project, either in the rainforest or cloudforests of Ecuador. The experience concludes with a six-week expedition through Peru, Bolivia and Chile.

Projects in Africa need volunteers to work for six weeks either on game reserves in Swaziland (ecological surveys, trail building) or in coastal villages in Tanzania (building schools, medical facilities). Both projects are followed by a six-week expedition through Swaziland, Mozambique, Botswana and Zambia, including a week's PADI scuba-diving course in Mozambique.

The six-week expeditions run independently over the summer.

Apply all the year round, preferably early in your last year at school. Teams of gap year students aged 18/19 leave throughout the year. No qualifications are needed, except for those wishing to work with children in Peru, where a good level of Spanish is required. A reasonable level of fitness is required. A sense of humour and willingness to work as part of a team is essential.

Expedition costs are from £3390-£3640, including board and accommodation, and support. Part of the costs go directly to the project. Flights and insurance are not included - applicants should budget from £550-£750 for these.

Contact: Quest Overseas, 32 Clapham Mansions, Nightingale Lane, London SW4 9AQ.
Tel: 020 8673 3313. Fax: 020 8673 7623.
Email: emailus@questoverseas.com
Website: www.questoverseas.com

Raleigh International   C/S

Raleigh International (formerly Operation Raleigh) is a charity that aims to develop young people by giving them the opportunity to carry out demanding environmental and community projects in the UK and around the world. Since 1984, 20,000 young people from 72 nations have taken part in over 190 expeditions in 35 countries.

Raleigh International will recruit 1000 young people, aged 17-25, from all walks of life, to undertake ten-week expeditions in Chile, Namibia, Ghana, Mongolia and Costa Rica and Nicaragua in 2001/ 2002, and also to Borneo, Sabah in 2003. Projects include building schools in northern Namibia and trekking above the snow line in southern Chile. Volunteers have the opportunity to travel on after the expedition independently.

To qualify for a place on a Raleigh International expedition, all participants take part in a weekend of demanding problem-solving and team-working challenges. Participants are asked to raise a contribution towards the cost of the programme, which covers their air fares and in-country expenses. The amount varies according to personal circumstances. A series of fundraising events is being organised and some bursaries are available.

Contact: Information Officer, Raleigh International, 27 Parson's Green Lane, London SW6 4HZ.

Tel: 020 7371 8585. Fax: 020 7371 5116.

Email: info@raleigh.org.uk

Website: www.raleigh.org

Profile Sue Wood
Chile with Raleigh International

'Gap years – everybody seemed to be taking them and I felt I was missing out. When I left school in 1994, it didn't occur to me to take time off before university. After my degree, a masters course and then work, I decided it was time to do something completely new and to see if I could cope in a foreign country, enduring physically demanding situations, meeting new people...would I be tough enough?

I looked at the various options and did a little research. I finally chose a Raleigh International expedition which allows you to combine environmental, community and adventure projects. The relationship Raleigh has with its host countries made me feel confident I would be able to make a positive and lasting contribution to the communities and the environment, long after I was home showing my photos! I was pleased to learn I would be able to work alongside local people.

So once I had chosen Raleigh, I needed it to choose me – to get on the three-month expedition to Patagonia in Southern Chile, I had to pass a demanding assessment weekend and raise £3000 to cover costs. At times I wondered if it was all worth it – months of raising money, buying all the equipment and organising a million and one things before I left. I also learnt some Spanish, and it paid off!

You don't find out what the projects will be until you are there, but you have a rough idea of what you are letting yourself in for after reading previous year's projects and attending a briefing weekend where you meet some of the people you will be with. My expedition started with sea kayaking, then radio-tracked a Chilean wildcat and finally building a fire station.

During the time I spent in Chile, I had some of the very best and the very worst experiences of my life. The friendships I made were intense and special. You are on the other side of the world, living in a tent, spending day and night together, putting up with each other's smells, eating together, singing songs, laughing harder than you thought possible – it is surprising how you are able to handle it all.

Situations arise that no one can prepare you for. One night we were woken to be told that the camp was flooding and we had two minutes to move to safety. Other experiences included taking my first English lesson with 30 children who could only say 'hello' and 'goodbye'; spending my first night in a bivouac shelter I made myself; kayaking for miles and then seeing a school of dolphins; standing in the middle of the rainforest at night waving an aerial above my head trying to detect wildcats; finishing the building of a firestation in a remote village; sitting in hot springs after not being able to wash for a week. These are among the memories I will treasure forever and are what makes the expedition one of the most challenging things I have ever done!

I originally went on the expedition to think about what I wanted to do with my life, but whilst away I used the time to make the most of the experience. When I returned home, I was more focused about my career and seized an opportunity that had been staring me in the face before I left...I just hadn't had the nerve to go for it before Raleigh!'

The Right Hand Trust

The Right Hand Trust offers a gap-year experience living and working in Africa. Volunteers should be aged 18-30, be practising Christians and be available for eight months or longer. The trip includes a three-week holiday. Placements are available in Kenya, Malawi, Namibia, Swaziland, the Gambia, Uganda, Zimbabwe and Zambia. Activities range from teaching, paramedical and social work to administration and vocational training. Training for the work takes place in the UK before departure.

Volunteers need to raise money through sponsorship and employment to finance the trip which costs around £2900 (this includes air fare, training, accommodation and insurance). Accommodation is simple and will probably be in a brick-built bungalow. There may not be electricity; water is probably from a standpipe and sanitation is communal. Furnishings are basic.

Contact: Right Hand Trust, Gelligason, Llanfair Caereinion, Powys SY21 9HE.

Tel: 01938 810215.

Website: www.righthandtrust.org.uk

Skillshare International   S (EXP)

Skillshare International offers opportunities for skilled, qualified, experienced and flexible people aged between 21 and the retirement age of the countries they work in, to work with placements from six months to two years in Africa and Asia. Areas of work include education, health, construction, agriculture, management and engineering. In some circumstances, partners and children can be accommodated. Candidates need to be qualified to at least HND level and have two years' work experience. They may apply for specific posts or for the general recruitment programme.

Successful candidates are provided with flights, NI payments, accommodation health insurance and receive an allowance, which is sufficient to maintain a reasonable standard of living.

Contact: Skillshare International, 126 New Walk, Leicester LE1 7JA.

Tel: 0116 254 1862. Fax: 0116 254 2614.

Email: info@skillshare.org

Website: www.skillshare.org

Students Partnership Worldwide (SPW)   C/S

SPW recruits volunteers aged 18-28 for educational, environmental and social programmes in India, Nepal, South Africa, Tanzania, Uganda and Zimbabwe. 50% of the volunteers are recruited locally in these countries. SPW volunteers live and work in a rural community alongside a young local volunteer. Together, they will build awareness of important social and environmental issues, such as HIV/Aids, soil erosion and sanitation, and will help members of the community begin to tackle these issues themselves. Programmes last for four to nine months.

SPW is a non-profit making charity – this means that volunteers are only asked to cover their own costs (£2600 - £2950).

Contact: Students Partnership Worldwide, 17 Dean's Yard, London SW1P 3PB.

Tel: 020 7222 0138. Fax: 020 7233 0008.

Email: spwuk@gn.apc.org

Website: www.spwuk.org

Profile   **Sarah Polack**

To Tanzania with SPW

'I wanted a break from studying after A levels and a year out seemed the perfect opportunity to pursue my interests in other countries, cultures and issues of development and conservation.

After reading through endless leaflets on all the many options open to potential 'year outers', I finally decided to apply to an environmental project with SPW (Students Partnership Worldwide). I spent the first six months of the year working to raise the money (I also managed to get some financial help by writing to various sponsors) and finally at the end of February I set off with fifteen other people to Dar-es-salaam.

The project involved a five-week training period in various parts of Tanzania, looking at and learning about the environmental and developmental issues. We then spent seven weeks in smaller groups living in villages in the Usambara mountains and worked alongside the local primary school and local farmers on environmental issues relevant to the immediate area. Our major projects included helping to set up a tree nursery at the school for village use and constructing steps on a severely eroding slope. We also spent some time with the children, trying to provide basic environmental education.

One of the really positive aspects of this project was that the group was made up of fifteen British and fifteen Tanzanian students. Two very different cultures coming together to live and work involved a lot of day-to-day compromises, but also a huge amount of fun and laughter. Great friendships were formed and I'm still in touch with many of the Tanzanian students.

It was a fascinating few weeks and opened my eyes to all sorts of development issues; the involvement of the Western World - both the positive and negative aspects. I learnt about a new culture so different from our own, and memories such as dancing on hill tops with local women, learning to cook chapatis on a little Chinese stove and the warm hospitality of our neighbours will travel with me forever.

After the project I then had the opportunity to travel for a while. I feel I gained from my six months not only the opportunity to become actively involved in some environmental work, but also a great deal of independence and ability to cope with unexpected and often bizarre situations.

Coming home was, in some way, harder than going there. I was of course very excited about seeing friends and family but after such an incredible six months I knew returning back to 'normality' wouldn't be easy. It wasn't easy, but so many people were eager to hear about *my time out there, and that helped keep alive what rapidly began to feel like a long dream. It takes time, but gradually it all fits into place and now magical memories hit me at the most unexpected moments and make even the most tedious lectures bearable!!'*

Sunseed Trust   C

Research and development work for enthusiastic volunteers in South-east Spain in the subjects of desert reclamation, tree planting, organic gardening and hydroponics, solar-cooker design, and other appropriate technology for desert areas; as well as education, publicity and fundraising, construction and maintenance, administration and management. The Trust also has links with similar placements in Tanzania.

Work is available for four weeks to one year full-time or one week to six weeks part-time. Costs range from £50 to £120. Apply at any time. More notice is needed in high season or if applicant has disabilities.

Contact: The Sunseed Trust, PO Box 2000, Cambridge CB4 3UJ.

Tel/Fax: 01926 421380 (bookings)

Website: www.sunseed.org.uk

Teaching Abroad   S

Teaching Abroad places volunteers to teach spoken English in China, Ghana, India, Mexico, Mongolia, Nepal, Peru, Russia, Romania, South Africa, Thailand, Togo and the Ukraine. The minimum stay is one month; three to four months is usual. Preferably apply one year in advance.

Applicants need to be over 17 at the time of travel, and to have university entrance qualifications and the capacity to rise to a challenge. Costs are upwards of £795.

Contact: Teaching & Projects Abroad, Gerrard House, Rustington, West Sussex BN16 1AW.

Tel: 01903 859911. Fax: 01903 785779

Email: info@teaching-abroad.co.uk

Website: www.teaching-abroad.co.uk

Tear Fund (Christian Action with the World's Poor)   S

Tearfund provides opportunities for single, evangelical Christians over the age of 18. Their four-month programme in Africa and Asia is designed for those taking a gap year. The programme runs from April to July. The cost is in the region of £1900 covering orientation and all other costs (excluding vaccinations). Other programmes last two to six weeks.

Contact: Tear Fund, 100 Church Road, Teddington, Middlesex TW11 8QE.

Tel: 0845 355 8355.

Email: enquiry@tearfund.org

Website: www.tearfund.org/transform

Travellers Worldwide   C/S

Volunteers teach conversational English/spoken English and or a specialised subject e.g. geography, maths, drama, sports etc in India, Sri Lanka, Nepal, South Africa, Russia or Ukraine. By living and working in a different country, volunteers learn their culture 'from the inside'. No formal teaching qualifications, or teaching experience, is required. Costs vary, according to the placement e.g. teaching in India costs £1095, excluding flights, for up to three months, plus £75 for each additional month. Accommodation and food is provided.

Conservation volunteers are recruited for placements in South Africa and Sri Lanka, for up to three months. Costs for three months is £1495 excluding flights, but including all food and accommodation.

Work experience placements are also available in South Africa, India, Sri Lanka and Russia. Examples of placements include in hotel/catering, tourism, law, journalism, medicine.

Placements are flexible in length, and can last for up to a year. Applicants should be at least 17 years (no upper age limit). The placements are open to all. It can be possible to combine two or more types of placement.

Contact: Travellers Worldwide, 7 Mulberry Close, Ferring, West Sussex BN12 5HY.

Tel: 01903 700478/502595. Fax: 01903 502595.

Email: phil@travellersworldwide.com

Website: www.travellersworldwide.com

Trekforce Expeditions   C/S

Trekforce offers an opportunity to play a part in international conservation. Trekforce runs 8 to 20 week expeditions in Belize, Central America and Sarawak, South East Asia, concentrating on endangered rainforests and working with the local communities. Their extended programmes of four to five months incorporate expedition work, learning new languages and teaching in rural communities such as the Kelabit of Sarawak or the Mayans of Belize. Experiences span from working as a team in demanding environments to working independently among different cultures. Those interested can find out more on one of their introduction days.

Contact: Trekforce Expeditions, 34 Buckingham Palace Road, London SW1W 0RE.

Tel: 020 7828 2275.

Email: info@trekforce.org.uk

Website: www.trekforce.org.uk

UNA Exchange   C/S

UNA Exchange offers opportunities for volunteers to work in over 1000 international volunteer projects in around 60 countries. Each placement lasts two to three weeks and most involve manual conservation and renovation work, though there are also some social work projects. The majority of projects are for over 18s, but there are also projects for those aged 15 and over. Volunteers must pay a fee of around £100, and arrange their own transport to the project. Food and accommodation are provided. Most projects take place during July and August, but there are projects available throughout the year.

Contact: send an A5 SAE to UNA Exchange, Temple of Peace, Cathays Park, Cardiff CF10 3AP.

Tel: 029 2022 3088.

Email: unaexchange@btinternet.com

Website: unaexchange.org

VentureCo Worldwide   C/S

VentureCo Worldwide offer four-month programmes in South America and the Himalayas, aimed at those taking a gap year. The programme consists of three phases: learning a skill; voluntary project work and undertaking an expedition.

Inca Venture: starts with three weeks in Quito, Ecuador, having tuition in Spanish plus opportunities to explore. This is followed by joining one of the two voluntary projects, for four weeks - one focused on work with orphaned, indigenous Indian children in Quito, the other a conservation/permaculture project on the Pacific coast. This is followed by an eight-week expedition, a 6000-km journey, including travel by jeep, mountain bike and canoe, from the headwaters of the Amazon to Machu Picchu. Each member of the expedition takes a turn at leading, under supervision.

Himalaya Venture: initially based in Agra near the Taj Mahal, the Venture starts with three weeks which consists of an introduction to spoken Hindi, and to the culture of India. The voluntary work phase takes place in the Rajastan desert, caring for children who are unable to attend mainstream schools, and working with other children as a mentor. The organisation is also involved with a community health programme in a more remote part of the desert. The final eight-week expedition uses a variety of means, including camels and rafts, to reach a tiger project at Bandhavgarh, where three weeks is spent working with wildlife rangers. A flight to Katmandhu brings the expedition to its climax with a three-week trek to the Everest base camp.

Gap-year applicants must be aged 17½ to 19 years, post A level studies, and graduate gap applicants must be aged 21+. Apply 12 months in advance. Selection is by interview. Costs are £4000, including international flights and all in-country costs.

Contact: VentureCo Worldwide Ltd, Pleck House, Middletown, Moreton Morrell, Warwickshire CV35 9AU.

Tel: 01926 651071. Fax: 01926 650120.

Email: mail@ventureco-worldwide.com

Website: www.ventureco-worldwide.com

Village Education Project (Kilimanjaro)   S

This project offers volunteers the opportunity to teach English and extra-curricular activities such as sport, art and music to village primary school children aged 7-14. Volunteers also accompany children on school outings to a National Park and to the Indian Ocean. Volunteers live as one of the villagers, in a village high on the slopes of Mount Kilimanjaro. Two weeks training is given prior to a January departure. Placements may last from eight months to a year. Costs are £1850 plus living expenses and insurance. Applicants should be educated to A level standard, be aged 18+ and speak English as their mother tongue, and should apply the April before departure the following January.

Contact: Village Education Project (Kilimanjaro), Mint Cottage, Prospect Road, Sevenoaks, Kent TN13 3UA.

Tel: 01732 459799.

Profile   **Sophie Ellis**

Teacher in Kilimanjaro with Village Education Project

'I remember the exact moment I decided I was going to take a gap year between school and university. It was on the plane, on the way back from visiting my brother who was teaching in South Africa. Seeing him having such an amazing, carefree time in a stunning country made me realise I couldn't miss out.

I started applying to every project I had heard of and got accepted for a couple, but something struck a chord when I received the

161

information from the Village Education Project - I just knew it was for me. I was ecstatic when, after my interview (which involved crawling around pretending to be a snake), I was accepted. I threw all my efforts into saving and fundraising. As I didn't leave until the January, I worked for seven months in the local council. I also had a fundraising dinner dance which raised over £800.

There were eight of us, living in a massive village quite high up on the slopes of Kilimanjaro. I taught the equivalent of reception class and the pupils learned their first words of English. Everyday I would wake up excited at the prospect of going to work - singing songs and laughing with the children - a stark contrast to now; waking up with a hangover in cold, wet Sheffield late for an uninspiring lecture.

People always say it must've taken a lot of guts to up and leave everything you know for eight months. This was nothing as hard as when I had to leave Tanzania. Those eight months were magical and it still brings tears to my eyes when I think of leaving the village and the children behind.

It's hard to sum up what the whole gap year was like. There were a few hard times when I missed home and just wanted things to be 'normal' again. However, the good times were indescribable - taking the children to the sea for the first time, drinking a cold beer on a deserted white beach in Zanzibar, reaching the top of Kilimanjaro after viewing it from my garden for six months, being charged by an elephant and having to run for my life...I could go on and on. I am aware that I probably bore my housemates at uni with my tales, but the memories are always with me, springing to my mind as fresh as if I was still there.

For those worried about settling back after taking a gap year, it has been hard for me with my new perspective on the world, but it's possible. Now, the most special times for me are when we all meet up and laugh about our crazy adventures or go on missions together either at home or on holiday. I wouldn't have missed out on any moment of it for the world!'

Voluntary Service Overseas (VSO)   *C/S (EXP)*

VSO recruits volunteers who work in the fields of education, natural resources, the health services, technical trades and engineering, business and social work. Work takes place in over 70 developing countries in Eastern and Central Europe, Africa, Asia and the Pacific.

VSO recruit those aged 20-68, and require professional qualifications and /or experience in most cases. The majority of placements are for two years. VSO pays fares and various grants, health insurance and

NI contributions. The overseas employer provides accommodation and a salary based on local rates.

VSO also runs a number of youth programmes, open to those aged 17-25. These programmes run alongside VSO's standard programme, and provide an opportunity for young people to become involved in overseas development work. One such programme is the Overseas Training Programme (OTP). This enables undergraduates to spend 10-12 months, between the second and third year of their degree course, gaining practical work experience in an overseas setting. OTP organises trainees' training, travel costs, living allowance etc; all trainees are expected to raise a £500 contribution towards the costs.

To gain an insight into what working overseas with VSO is really like, call 0845 603 0027, 6pm-9pm weekdays (local rates) to talk to someone who's already done it.

Contact: VSO Enquiries Unit, 317 Putney Bridge Road, London SW15 2PN.

Tel: 020 8780 7500. Fax: 020 8780 7300.

Email: enquiry@vso.org.uk

Website: www.vso.org.uk

Profile   **Emily Polack**

Working on a development project in Cambodia with VSO's Overseas Training Programme

'I am studying development and I wanted to have first hand experience of issues being faced by different people in developing countries and of the range of 'solutions' being tried and tested. I decided to take a year out before the final year of my degree to enable me to gain a greater understanding of the issues I am studying and to gain the practical experience needed for finding work in development after graduating. I also hoped to make a contribution in some way to the work of a development organisation. The Overseas Training Programme suited my needs.

I have been working with a local non-governmental organisation in Ratanakiri, Cambodia for 10 months. The project is called NTFP (Non-Timber Forest Products) and is mainly involved with natural resource management by indigenous communities. In Ratanakiri, indigenous people are the majority and there are seven different ethnic groups all speaking different languages. Through their animist beliefs, their cultivation systems and livelihoods are closely connected to the natural world around them.

The NTFP project is assisting communities to develop community-based solutions to protect and manage their natural resources in the face of external threats and conventional economic development. It also aims to support indigenous people to increase their participation in relevant policy-making.

Having had very little knowledge or experience of natural resource management or indigenous issues, the most useful skills that I could bring initially were office-based ones, in particular English language/report writing. Engaging in this type of work was a good way to find out about the project and related issues past and present. I found I had to keep an open mind and have a readiness to learn.

During my time in Cambodia, I have been responsible for communications with other organisations working in natural resources. I have written English papers for conferences and workshops and assisted in setting up documentation systems to make information more accessible and to increase community ownership of projects. I have also been working with a group of indigenous young people on research related to the impacts of a hydropower dam in Vietnam.

Ten months into my gap year, I feel I have developed a good understanding of the situation of indigenous communities in Ratanakiri and their rights. I also feel I have gained a range of experience in development issues and have been inspired to learn more about sustainable agriculture. I have also learned practical office skills such as publishing programs and information systems.'

Winant Clayton Volunteer Association S

This organisation offers a cross cutural voluntary exachange programme between the UK and USA. Each summer, approximately 20 volunteers go to the USA East coast to work in local community projects. The placements are in a range of settings – working with children; with people with HIV/AIDS; the elderly; people with disabilities; in mental health; with the homeless. The experience offers the chance for personal development by the challenge of living abroad and working in quite challenging areas. Volunteers spend three months away – eight weeks working and two/three weeks for travel. The preferred application period is September to January; interviews are held in February. Volunteers are provided with free accommodation and an allowance. Volunteers pay their own airfare, insurance and visa costs – about £380, and they need money for travelling. Experience of voluntary work is desirable but not essential. Candidates need to demonstrate that they have some understanding of voluntary work, and that they will gain from the experience. Good team and communication skills are important.

Contact: Winant Clayton Volunteer Association, The Davenant Centre, 179 Whitechapel Road, London E1 1DU.

Tel: 020 7375 0547.

Email: wcva@dircon.co.uk

Website: www.wcva.dircon.co.uk

World Challenge Expeditions   C/S

Their Gap Challenge programme offers opportunities for voluntary work, from two to nine months, ranging from teaching in Tanzania to conservation work in the rainforests of Belize. Some paid work is also available, as are various expeditions (see chapters 9,13).

Contact: World Challenge Expeditions, Black Arrow House, 2 Chandos Road, London NW10 6NF.

Tel: 020 8728 7272.

Email: welcome@world-challenge.co.uk

Website: www.world-challenge.co.uk

Worldwide Volunteering for Young People (formerly Youth for Britain)

Worldwide Volunteering for Young People (formerly Youth for Britain) is a registered charity offering a computer database of volunteering opportunities for young people. The Worldwide Volunteering database is a comprehensive source of information on full-time volunteering for 16 to 25-year-olds, enabling volunteers to match their wishes against the requirements of volunteer organisations. Users build a profile on screen of their ideal placement and this is then matched against some 800 organisations with over 250,000 annual placements throughout the UK and 214 countries overseas. Projects last anything from a week to a year or more. The database is available in many schools, careers centres, volunteer bureaux etc. – so ask locally, or apply to the address below for a questionnaire.

Contact: Worldwide Volunteering for Young People, Higher Orchard, Sandford Orcas, Sherborne, Dorset DT9 4RP.

Tel/fax: 01963 220036.

Email: yfb@worldvol.co.uk

Website: www.worldwidevolunteering.org.uk

WWOOF UK part of World Wide Opportunities on Organic Farms   C

There are opportunities for members to work on organic farms and smallholdings throughout Europe and beyond. WWOOF UK provides advice and a contacts list; the rest is up to the member and host.

For full details see the entry in chapter 7.

Youth Action for Peace UK   **W**

Volunteers aged 18+ work at summer projects and international workcamps for two to three weeks, paying their own travel expenses and an application and membership fee. Projects vary from tree planting in Ghana to organising a folk festival in Belgium. Participants with special needs are welcome. YAP also organises voluntary projects in Britain. YAP International organises seminars and training courses on human rights, multicultural issues etc. Apply from April onwards.

Contact: Youth Action for Peace UK, 8 Golden Ridge, Freshwater, Isle of Wight PO40 9LE.

Tel: 01983 752557. Fax: 01983 756900.

Email: yapuk@ukonline.co.uk

Website: www.yap-uk.org

Chapter 11
Using your time to learn and study abroad

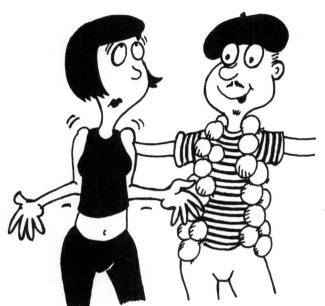

Why not consider using part, or all, of your year out to develop your skills, or learn about new cultures and ways of life in other countries? You could spend time living with a family in a foreign country, attending a local school or taking a short course at a university. Or take the opportunity to develop your foreign language skills on a course abroad. You could choose to spend a whole year studying in an EU member state as part of your higher education course.

Undertaking such activities can bring you into contact with people of different nationalities, broaden your horizons, and help you to learn more about other cultures, and yourself.

The opportunities for learning and study abroad described in this chapter have been grouped as follows:

- study abroad during/after school or college
- paying guest, homestays and exchange visits
- developing your foreign language skills
- developing sporting/outdoor pursuits skills
- study abroad as part of your higher education course.

Studying abroad during/after school or college

There are opportunities to spend up to a year in another country, living with a host family and attending school there, or undertaking short courses at a university. Lower age limits vary from 15 to 18 years. A few programmes have an upper age limit of 18. Destinations include the USA and other English-speaking countries, and also non-English-speaking countries, allowing you to develop your language skills. Costs vary, as do the durations of programmes - from a few weeks to an academic year.

Another option for learning is to join an educational tour, and learn more about topics such as art or the natural environment.

A number of these programmes are described in the following section.

AFS International Youth Development

AFS International Youth Development is a non-profit-making voluntary organisation. It arranges for 16-18-year olds to spend a year in one of 55 different countries (or six-month placements in certain countries) living as a member of a family and going to a local secondary school. Young people in Britain who take part in the programme usually go after GCSEs or A levels/vocational A levels/ BTEC, or after equivalent qualifications in Scotland.

Before going abroad, young people attend orientation sessions in the UK where discussions take place regarding adapting to life in another country. In the country they go to they will also attend an introductory language course and they will be allocated to a local AFS counsellor who they can contact with any questions or problems.

AFS students can go to a variety of countries in Europe (e.g. France, Italy, Norway and Slovakia) and further afield (e.g. Bolivia, Brazil, Chile, Colombia, Honduras, Indonesia, Panama, Paraguay, Thailand, the USA and Venezuela). Each year, AFS in the UK agrees links with certain countries and will then send its students there. The countries available can change each year but, if a student is interested in studying in a particular country, AFS will try to make arrangements to send the young person there. Those interested in going to Brazil, France, Indonesia, Italy, Norway, Paraguay, Slovakia, the USA and Venezuela should apply by 31 October to depart the following June/July/August. They will return in June/July after a twelve-month programme. Early application is advisable for any country (i.e. well before the closing date) as the programmes are popular.

It is also possible to do a six-month placement in Honduras, Brazil, Peru, Guatemala, Ecuador, Panama, Costa Rica or South Africa. Students can apply throughout the year with departures in January and July. Full-year programmes to these countries can also be arranged and application should be made before 31 October.

Students will be able to experience a new country and culture and to learn a new language. They will also gain in independence, self-confidence and maturity and will make international friends.

The cost of going on an AFS programme (2001/02) is £3950 for a year and £2950 for six months, which includes travel, support, insurance, medical cover, language help, orientation in the UK prior to the visit, accommodation with a family and activities during the year. £500-£1000 spending money will also be needed. AFS does, however, offer financial assistance on a means-tested basis. Those who are going to apply for financial assistance should do so early as demand is high. AFS is keen to make sure that lack of finance is not a factor which prevents young people from taking part in the programme. Substantial fundraising support is also given.

Contact: AFS International Youth Development, Leeming House, Vicar Lane, Leeds LS2 7JF.

Tel: 0845 458 2101. Fax: 0845 458 2102.

Email: info-unitedkingdom@afs.org

Website: www.afsuk.org

Profile **Helen Philips**

To Brazil with AFS International Youth Development

'Now I have come back from my worthwhile experience in Brazil!

At the beginning, it was hard to be part of my host family. They had a deaf daughter and she was fifteen years old.

My project at the deaf school had been fun. I was helping teach drama for all ages of deaf students, and I was the first deaf person going into the school to help with teaching. The young deaf children thought I was hearing and I said "I am deaf the same as you". They didn't believe me, but after a while they all realised that I was deaf and got on well with me!

It was hard to teach the young deaf children drama, and trying to get their attention all the time, but it was really fun. At the end of the year, they all did a Christmas presentation. So did I. I worked as the director and prompter, with five-year-old deaf children doing signing and singing. Everyone was gobsmacked because there was no hearing person helping us do it. They asked me if I could hear the music, and I said "No, I am profoundly deaf", and they couldn't believe it.

Previously the older deaf students copied the hearing teacher while they were doing the signing singing. I proved to them that they can do it without the hearing teacher helping them.

169

There were no facilities for deaf people in Santa Rosa, for example, they don't have the minicom, interpreter, and there is no equal opportunity there, and everything is so expensive for them to buy the facilities.

I have made loads of deaf friends and my Brazilian signing got better in about one month, but learning Portuguese had been really hard and confusing, and it was fun.

I believe more deaf people should go to Brazil, or other countries, because while I was there I was the role model, and showed the hearing teacher what the deaf can do. It had been hard for me, but it was so successful at the end, I advise all deaf young people to go abroad to see the real thing and the culture, and show that deaf and hearing are equal.

In my last week, I realised six months had gone by, and I was returning home. I felt that I didn't want to go back to England, because I had made loads of great friends in Brazil - but it was time for me to leave the host family.

They all gave me a surprise farewell party. About 35 people came to the party, and it was really nice, but sad leaving them.

I will go back to Brazil in about three or four years' time to see all of them again.'

AHA (Art History Abroad)

AHA offers the chance to broaden your horizons by studying the masterpieces of European art in Venice, Florence and Rome. The course lasts six weeks, in autumn or spring, and can form part of your gap year. All tuition takes place on site in small tutor groups of eight, lead by a young expert. There are also two-week summer courses. Fees include accommodation, flights, museum entrance fees; all travel in Italy and tuition. Limited to 24 students.

Contact: AHA Courses Ltd, 26 Delaune Street, London SE17 3UU.

Tel/Fax: 020 7582 8082.

Email: info@arthistoryabroad.com

Website: www.arthistoryabroad.com

American Institute for Foreign Study (AIFS)

Operates the Academic Year in America Program. This is for young people aged between 15 and 18½. Participants stay with an American family and attend high school for a year.

Contact: AFIS, 37 Queen's Gate, London SW7 5HR.

Tel: 020 7581 7300.

Website: www.aifs.com

EIL - Cultural and Educational Travel

EIL is a charity specialising in cultural and educational travel, established in the USA in 1932, running a wide variety of programmes. Through their Community College Programme USA, students aged 18+ may attend an American Community College for five or ten months.

Contact: EIL, 287 Worcester Road, Malvern, Worcestershire WR14 1AB.
Tel: 01684 562577. Fax: 01684 562212.

Email: info@eiluk.org

Website: www.eiluk.org

The English-Speaking Union of the Commonwealth

This organisation offers scholarships for post A level students to spend two or three academic terms at American and Canadian independent schools. Scholarships begin in September and January. Students must have good general academic ability and show an interest in North American culture and society. Scholars are asked to pay their own air fare, insurance and incidental expenses.

Contact: The Education Officer, The English-Speaking Union, Dartmouth House, 37 Charles Street, London W1J 5ED.
Tel: 020 7529 1550. Fax: 020 7495 6108.

Email: heather_wain@esu.org

Website: www.esu.org.uk

European Educational Opportunities Programme (EEOP) and International Educational Opportunities Programme (IEOP)

Provides academic year programmes in schools in Europe and in high schools, colleges and universities in America for students aged between 15 and 18½. Also arranges homestays for upwards of two weeks. Costs vary.

Contact: EEOP & IEOP, 122 Canterbury Road, Lydden, Dover CT15 7ET.
Tel: 01304 830948. Fax: 01304 831914.

Email: suebugden@eeop.com

Website: www.eeop.com

The Fulbright Commission

The US Educational Advisory Service at the Fulbright Commission provides information on courses and exchange programmes in the USA. It produces information sheets on study abroad programmes for secondary school students, exchange programmes with the US and gap-year study in the US. It holds 800 prospectuses and American college guides, and information on work exchanges. The Commission can also give advice to those wanting to study for an entire degree course in the US and the scholarships available.

Contact: US Educational Advisory Service, The Fulbright Commission, Fulbright House, 62 Doughty Street, London WC1N 2JZ.

Tel: 020 7404 6994. Fax: 020 7404 6874.

Email: education@fulbright.co.uk

Website: www.fulbright.co.uk

The Hebrew University of Jerusalem's Rothberg International School

The Hebrew University Gap Year programme is popular with gap-year students. Running from January to June, it combines field work, study tours, classes and many social and cultural activities. Classes include Hebrew language instruction and topics related to Israeli culture and politics.

Full-year courses are also available for school leavers, undergraduates and graduates, and short-term summer and language courses are also offered. Financial assistance may be available.

Contact: The Hebrew University of Jerusalem's Rothberg International School, c/o UK Student Department, Friends of the Hebrew University, 126 Albert Street, London NW1 7NE.

Tel: 020 7691 1478

Email: students@fhu.org.uk

Website: www.huji.ac.il

John Hall Pre-University Interim Course

John Hall offers courses in Italy for non-specialists, on European civilisation, especially the visual arts and music, including architecture, conservation, opera, design, literature and Italian cinema. They include practical options: Italian language, drawing, painting and photography. Spring course: introductory week in London followed by six weeks in Venice where accommodation, meals, lectures, visits and classes are included in the cost: £5210, with optional extra periods in Florence and Rome.

Contact: The Secretary, John Hall Pre-University Course, 12 Gainsborough Road, Ipswich, Suffolk IP4 2UR.

Tel: 01473 251223. Fax: 01473 288009.

Website: www.johnhallpre-university.com

The Smallpeice Trust

The Smallpeice Engineering Careers Foundation Year (ECFY) provides basic engineering and associated skills which will make students immediately useful and hence employable at the end of their degree. The programme is divided into three parts:

- three months' academic study at a UK university
- one month language tuition at a European language school
- three months' work placement in one of nine countries in Europe.

The programme is open to students aged 18+, who must hold a deferred place on an engineering-related degree course. The deadline for applications is 31 October for the following September start. The programme costs £30 per week.

Contact: The Smallpeice Trust, 74 Upper Holly Walk, Leamington Spa, Warwickshire CV32 4JL.

Tel: 01926 333200. Fax: 01926 333202.

Email: gen@smallpeicetrust.org.uk

Website: www.smallpeicetrust.org.uk

The Wilderness Trust

Provides experiential learning opportunities with associated organisations in South Africa, Norway and Alaska. Opportunities may last from five days to three months, and are suitable for gap-year students. Primitive, minimum impact walking trails in wilderness areas are arranged with small groups of no more than eight people. You need to be generally fit and over 16 years of age. More information on these opportunities is available on the Trust's website.

Contact: The Wilderness Trust, The Oast House, Near Pevensey, East Sussex BN24 5AP.

Tel: 01323 461730. Fax: 01323 761913.

Email: info@wilderness-trust.org

Website: www.wilderness-trust.org

Profile **Clare Robinson**

Army Cadet Force South African expedition with the Wilderness Trust

'As soon as we arrived in South Africa, the first thing we noticed was the kindness of the people. Everyone waved at us while we were travelling and whenever we stopped we soon discovered that we had attracted a small crowd.

173

The first part of the expedition was the 'Zulu culture experience'. This was where we had our first real taste of this remarkable country and its equally remarkable people. After a full day of travelling, we finally arrived at Simunye Lodge. Here, we left our kit in a truck and rode down into a beautiful valley on horseback, where we were greeted by two Zulu women who were cooking around a fire.

We set off on what we thought would be a long walk to a campsite. By this time, it was the dark hour which was the time between the sun going down and the moon coming up. The sky was beginning to reveal its many stars. Even the stars looked different as we were in the Southern Hemisphere.

Whilst we were walking, we suddenly heard singing and the beating of drums. Then we were faced with about fifteen Zulu men and boys running down the hillside towards us. At first we were all shocked as we had no idea what to expect.

We followed the Zulus, who carried on singing until we reached their village. The village was beautiful and had small rooms made from stone set into the hillside. A river ran straight through the middle of the valley with an old wooden bridge stretched across it. That night we all sat around a campfire after a display of Zulu dancing.

The next day, we left for the battlefield tours, which gave us an insight into the famous Zulu wars. The guides told their stories with such enthusiasm that it was possible to believe you were actually there, watching the battles go on in front of you.

For me, the best part of the expedition was to come next - the wilderness trails in the Umfolozi game reserve and the Lake St Lucia wetlands, run by the Wilderness Leadership School. At first I was dubious, as we were told that they would be 'trails of self-discovery' and that they would probably change our outlook on life. However, I found this to be very true.

The only other living things we came across during the trails were the plants and animals. Everything we needed to survive was carried on our backs. We would walk during the day and often stop for a siesta when it was too hot to walk. We would find a campsite before the sun set each night. Each morning, when we left, we would leave nothing behind but our footprints. It would not even be possible to tell where we had had a fire. This was called 'minimum impact camping'.

Our group of nine, including the guide, became very close during this phase. One of my many memorable experiences was when we were all sat around the campfire under the light of the moon and stars, discussing the day while waiting for our supper to cook. Suddenly, we were all halted by the most overpowering and heartstopping noise I have ever heard in my life, the long and amazing roar of a lion. As we all sat, wide-eyed and trying to listen harder, we gradually heard another lion answer, then another, then another, coming from all directions and distances in the reserve.

This was truly wonderful. I had found what I wanted to find in Africa; a new outlook. I realised that I was one human sat in South Africa at night, and I was totally surrounded by such overwhelming animals. Never before have I been to a country where humans aren't in control, even of nature. But here, we were in the animals' habitat. They were in control, and we had to respect them and their homes. It felt scary but, somehow, it felt right.

Every night, each group member would have to do one hour of nightwatch, where you were the only person awake and everyone else was really depending on you. This meant keeping the fire going, which was our only protection from the wild animals, other than the guide's rifle. Despite close encounters with rhino, buffalo, hippo and giraffe, I soon began to look forward to my nightwatch, as I realised it was the most valuable time, when I could sit on my own beneath the stars and think about absolutely anything.

During this phase, not only did I learn practical skills but, more importantly, I learned about myself. I discovered my own feelings and limitations and had a lot of time to think about where I want to go in life and what I want to achieve.

The next phase was our Duke of Edinburgh Gold Award expedition in the Drakensberg mountains, a tremendous and exhilarating challenge. We reached peaks of about 8000 feet. I felt the effects of the altitude, as my nose started bleeding on several surprise occasions. One night, we found ourselves sleeping in temperatures of -15 degrees on an exposed mountain plain. This in itself was an experience, especially when trying to put up shelters and cook food with freezing, numb hands.

Even though you were stood at 8000 feet and could see for what looked like forever, you could still see no signs of civilisation. No roads, no pylons, no people - just pure wilderness. All you can hear is the wind, the animals and each other. I have tried my hardest to imagine being able to do that anywhere in England.

The final phase was extremely rewarding. We provided facilities and coaching for two local primary schools and one secondary school. However, it appeared that we coached them too well, as we organised a tournament for the final day and the children beat us at everything except cricket. To thank us, they put on a show of dancing and singing.

At the end of the expedition, we were all sad to be leaving, but happy with what we were leaving behind and with the experiences and memories we were taking with us. I have had the most life-changing experience, and have learned so much.'

WorldNetUK

Study programmes:

Educare is for 18 to 26-year-olds to study part-time at college or university whilst living with an American family and acting as a companion to their school age children. Participants must have held a full driving licence for at least six months and have some practical experience with children aged six years or over.

Academic Year America is for 15 to 18-year-olds to spend either one term or a full academic year attending a US High School and living with an American family. Departures are in August and January. The programme is sponsored by the American Institute for Foreign Study.

Contact: WorldNetUK, Central Office, Emerton House, 26 Shakespeare Road, Bedford MK40 2ED.
Tel: 07002 287247. Fax: 01234 351070.

Email: info@worldnetuk.com
Website: www.worldnetuk.com

Youth for Understanding (YFU)

YFU is a private, non-profit-making, long-established international educational exchange organisation. YFU's core programme is an educational exchange experience. Each year, it operates approximately 190 programmes and about 8,000 students from around the world participate in them.

YFU encourages parents to become involved by being host parents and encourages students to widen their horizons as exchange students experiencing the everyday life, language and culture in their chosen country. Exchange students from the UK can go to the USA, Europe, Canada and New Zealand for a year, live with a (carefully selected) host family and attend school there. Exchanges to Australia will also soon be in operation. Students who choose a European country will spend time learning the language and may come back able to speak it fluently. Students attend a residential weekend of training before they leave and there is also further training in the host country. YFU also provides caring support to students throughout the year.

The exchange programme is open to young people aged 16-18, or aged between 17-23 for the Community College Programme, who want to experience a new culture and gain maturity and language ability. Programme fees for participants include orientation, insurance, travel and support/counselling in the receiving country. Early application is advisable.

Contact: YFU UK, 15 Hawthorn Road, Erskine, Renfrewshire PA8 7BT.
Tel/Fax: 0141 812 5561.
Email: yfu@holliday123.freeserve.co.uk

Paying guests, homestays and exchange visits

These are short-term opportunities, offering you the chance to stay with another family abroad and learn about their way of life. If you are in a non-English-speaking country, it also provides a chance to develop your foreign language skills. Organisations which find host families will try to match you with a suitable family; reputable organisations will select host families carefully.

Staying as a paying guest with a family, also referred to as undertaking a homestay, means (as the name implies) that you pay for your accommodation. Paying guest or homestay visits last typically from one to four weeks, and can be combined with study.

Exchange visits are normally between two young people of a similar age who are still in education. They usually spend two weeks or more in each other's homes. Accommodation and food in the host country are usually free and the family often organises trips to see places of interest. A home-to-home exchange is a cheaper way of taking part in the life of a family abroad, and allows you to return their hospitality.

Organisations arranging exchanges and homestays are listed below; see also the Fulbright Commission earlier in this chapter.

Central Bureau for International Education and Training

The Central Bureau for International Education and Training can put schools and colleges in touch with partners abroad for the purpose of exchanges.

Contact: The Central Bureau for International Education and Training, The British Council, 10 Spring Gardens, London SW1A 2BN.
Tel: 020 7389 4004. Fax: 020 7389 4426.
Email: centralbureau@britishcouncil.org
Website: www.britishcouncil.org/cbiet/

EIL - Cultural and Educational Travel

As described earlier in this chapter, EIL specialises in cultural and educational travel. Their programmes include Individual Homestay placements, providing participants with an insight into the culture of a country. The Homestay programme is open to all age groups, for periods of up to four weeks, to more than 30 countries.

Contact: EIL, 287 Worcester Road, Malvern, Worcestershire WR14 1AB.
Tel: 01684 562577. Fax: 01684 562212.
Email: info@eiluk.org
Website: www.eiluk.org

En Famille Overseas

En Famille Overseas specialises in paying-guest visits to host families in France and Spain. Also language courses/one-to-one tuition with homestay in Paris, Tours, Nantes, La Rochelle, Le Havre, etc and Granada, Spain.

Contact: En Famille Overseas, The Old Stables, 60b Maltravers Street, Arundel, West Sussex BN18 9BG.

Tel: 01903 883266. Fax: 01903 883582.

Email: enfamilleoversea@aol.com

Euroyouth Abroad

Euroyouth Abroad works in cooperation with a number of continental youth travel organisations and with schools and colleges. As well as running programmes in the UK for young people from overseas, it also sends UK residents to a number of European countries for short stays abroad. Countries include Austria, Belgium, France, Greece, Italy, the Netherlands, Portugal and Spain. It can arrange for students to stay with families in Europe either as holiday guests or paying guests. Holiday guests undertake to make English conversation with the hosts and their children for about three to four hours daily. Paying guests go to speak the language of the host country and pay the family for their stay.

The periods arranged through Euroyouth Abroad are for short stays only, although some participants arrange further activities/employment in the country afterwards, independently of Euroyouth Abroad.

Contact: Euroyouth Abroad, 301 Westborough Road, Westcliff, Southend-on-Sea, Essex SSO 9PT.

Tel: 01702 341434. Fax: 01702 330104.

Experiment France

Experiment France was founded in 1934 following the creation of the 'Experiment in International Living' in the United States in 1932. Today, Experiment France is a not-for-profit organisation, with partners all over the world. The organisation is known to be one of the leaders in France for international and educational exchange programmes. Experiment France is now also a member of the Federation of International Youth Travel Organizations (FIYTO).

In France, Experiment France is a member of UNSE and L'OFFICE, which both gather information on exchange programmes organisations in order to promote a chart of quality. Experiment France is committed to the betterment of the quality of the services it provides.

All their programmes promote cross-cultural understanding at a very personal level, encouraging individual growth, global awareness and long lasting relationships. Participants, host family members and the selected schools have the opportunity to learn from each other, as they share within these programmes different lifestyles and cultural perspectives.

In keeping with these objectives, Experiment France can provide the following programmes: homestays for individuals; high school or boarding school programmes; intensive language courses (all year round); language courses at universities; paid internships; group programmes.

All programmes include the following features: the large number of cities where Experiment France is represented in France; the comprehensive nature of the programmes; the quality of the language schools involved; supervision and monitoring.

Contact: Experiment France, 89 rue de Turbigo, 75003 Paris, France

Tel: 00 33 1 4454 5800. Fax: 00 33 1 4454 5801.

Email: contact@experiment-france.org

Website: www.experiment-france.org

Travellers Worldwide

Apart from their voluntary placements described in chapter 10, Travellers Worldwide offer Cultural Exchange Programmes and Learning Spanish Programmes in Cuba. Participants live on a university campus, interacting with Cuban students and students of other nationalities. Prices are from £1,195 excluding flights, but including food and accommodation, for one, two or three months.

Contact: Travellers Worldwide, 7 Mulberry Close, Ferring, West Sussex BN12 5HY.

Tel: 01903 700478/502595. Fax: 01903 502595.

Email: phil@travellersworldwide.com

Website: www.travellersworldwide.com

Developing your foreign language skills

Any time spent in a non-English-speaking country will help you to develop your foreign language skills. This is especially true if you are living and mixing with local people, and take the opportunity to communicate as much as possible with others in their language.

Taking a course at a language school abroad is an option to consider. There are many organisations offering short language courses abroad; these advertise in the national press. The following list gives some examples of course providers.

Alliance Française, 1 Dorset Square, London NW1 6PU.
Tel: 020 7723 6439.
Email: info@aflondon.org.uk
Website: www.alliancefrancaise.org.uk
Runs French courses in London, France and worldwide.

CESA Languages Abroad, Western House, Malpas, Truro, Cornwall
TR1 1SQ. Tel: 01872 225300. Fax: 01872 225400.
Email: info@cesalanguages.com
Website: www.cesalanguages.com
Offer gap-year language courses from eight to 16 weeks and short courses from one to six weeks duration in Europe, South America, Japan etc. Course dates start throughout the year.

Council on International Educational Exchange (Council
Exchanges), 52 Poland Street, London W1V 4JQ. Tel: 020 7478 2020.
Fax: 020 7478 7322.
Email: infoUK@councilexchanges.org.uk
Website: www.councilexchanges.org.uk
Their Language Study Abroad programme offers a range of immersion language study options at schools in France, Germany, Italy, Spain, Ecuador or Cuba. Programmes range from two to 36 weeks and can be tailored to the participant. Accommodation ranges from 'home stay' to hotels.

EF International Language Schools, 1-3 Farman Street, Hove, East
Sussex BN3 1AL. Tel: 01273 201420.
Email: ils.uk.agents@ef.com
Website: www.ef.com
EF runs language courses abroad, both short-term and up to nine months.

Euro Academy, 24 Clarenden Rise, London SE13 5EY. Tel: 020 8297
0505. Email: enquiries@euroacademy.co.uk
Website: www.euroacademy.co.uk
Offer those aged 18+ language study courses abroad, for one to four weeks, in a number of European countries, Russia and Ecuador. Also offer work experience programmes in France and Germany.

Experiment France, 89 Rue de Turbigo, 75003 Paris, France.
Tel: 00 33 1 4454 58 00.
Runs various language programmes in institutions and universities in France. See their entry earlier in this chapter for more information about the organisation.

International House, *106 Piccadilly, London W1V 9FL. Tel: 020 7518 6900.*

Website:www.ihlondon.com

Runs language courses in London and at affiliated schools abroad.

Travellers Worldwide

Provide opportunities to learn Spanish in Cuba. See their earlier entry under 'paying guest, homestays and exchange visits' in this chapter.

Developing sporting/outdoor pursuits skills

Flying Fish

Flying Fish trains watersports' enthusiasts to professional levels in yachting, dinghy sailing, windsurfing, surfing and diving. Besides locations in the UK, courses are held in Greece and Australia. Courses are held all year round, and last from two weeks to twelve months. Applicants must be aged 18 by completion of the course. Experience in your chosen watersport is beneficial, but not essential. Many participants gain subsequent jobs through Flying Fish.

Contact: Flying Fish, 25 Union Road, Cowes, Isle of Wight PO31 7TW.

Tel: 01983 280641. Fax: 01983 281821.

Email: carol.dye@flyingfishonline.com

Website: www.flyingfishonline.com

Peak Leaders

Offers ski and snowboard instructor courses in the Canadian Rockies and Argentina; these include instructor and leader accreditation, mountain safety, first aid and avalanche awareness certification, and formal management training (NEBS Introductory Team Leader Award). Adventure pursuits instructor courses are offered in Canada (canoeing, whitewater rafting, expedition planning, navigation), Indonesia (jungle leadership and watersports) and America (surfing).

Courses last from four to 12 weeks; apply as early as possible – preferably a year in advance. Costs vary according to the programme. For winter courses, students should be intermediate, or better, skiers or snowboarders. For summer courses, students should be able to swim. All students should be physically fit and mentally resilient.

Contact: Peak Leaders UK Ltd, Mansfield, Strathmiglo, Fife, Scotland KY14 7QE.

Tel/fax: 01337 860079.

Email: info@peakleaders.co.uk

Website: www.peakleaders.co.uk

Ski le Gap

Offers opportunities for students aged 18+ to qualify as ski or snowboard instructors, gaining either a Level I or Level II internationally recognised CSIA qualification. Training takes place at Mont Tremblant in Quebec. Courses last three months, or one month for a short course. Apply 12 months prior to starting.

Contact: Ski le Gap, PO Box 474, Mont Tremblant, Quebec JOT 120, Canada.

Tel: 0800 328 0345

Email: gap@citenet.net

Website: www.skilegap.com

Study abroad as part of your higher education course

ERASMUS

Instead of (or as well as!) spending time abroad before or after your higher education, there are many opportunities to undertake part of your higher education course in another EU country. This is possible through the ERASMUS programme, which is part of the Socrates European Community action programme. Under ERASMUS, it is possible to study at an institution in another participating European country (see website for current list) for between three months and a year. The study you undertake during that year is fully recognised as part of your higher education course. UK higher education institutions can provide details about the ERASMUS programmes in which they participate. If you are currently looking at various degree courses, find out which offer the opportunity for study through ERASMUS. Individual higher education institutions can provide information, or information can be obtained from the UK SOCRATES-ERASMUS Council.

Details of which higher education institutions have links with which countries can be found in the annual publication *Experience Erasmus – The UK Guide to SOCRATES-ERASMUS programmes* available in careers centres or from ISCO Publications, 12A Princess Way, Camberley, GU15 3SP.

For further information about EU programmes related to higher education, consult the DfES booklet *The European Choice - A Guide to Opportunities for Higher Education in Europe*, available in careers centres or from DfES Publications, tel: 0845 60 222 60.

Contact: UK SOCRATES-ERASMUS Council, Research & Development Building, The University of Kent, Canterbury, Kent CT2 7PD.
Tel: 01227 762712. Fax: 01227 762711.
Email: erasmus@ukc.ac.uk
Website: www.erasmus.ac.uk

The Smallpeice Trust

See the entry earlier in this chapter, describing the Smallpeice Engineering Careers Foundation Year (ECFY), which offers a learning and work placement package for students holding a deferred place on an engineering-related degree course.

Additional sources of information on study abroad

Apart from contacting embasssies (see list of addresses in Appendix 1), there are other organisations with bases in the UK which can provide information about studying in certain countries:

Austrian Cultural Institute

Provides information on the culture, economics and geography of Austria as well as information on studying in higher education in Austria and language courses. It has a library that is open to the public.

Contact: Austrian Cultural Institute, 28 Rutland Gate, London SW7 1PQ

Tel: 020 7584 8653. Fax: 020 7225 0470.

Email: culture@austria.org.uk

Website: www.austria.org.uk/culture

Finnish Institute in London

Provides information on international programmes taught in Finnish universities, student and staff exchanges and research grants and scholarships to Finland. The insitute also gives out information on where to study Finnish in the UK.

Contact: Finnish Institute in London, 35-36 Eagle Street, London WC1R 4AJ

Tel: 020 7404 3309. Fax: 020 7404 8893

Website: www.finnish-institute.org.uk

The Hispanic and Luso Brazilian Council

Information leaflets costing £4 each are available on study courses, opportunities and employment in Spain, Portugal and Latin America. Library open to members and the general public.

Contact: The Hispanic and Luso Brazilian Council, Canning House, 2 Belgrave Square

London SW1X 8PJ

Tel: 020 7235 2303

Email: education@canninghouse.com

Website: www.canninghouse.com

The Italian Cultural Institute

Provides general information on Italy plus information on working, studying and attending Italian language classes in Italy. For information write in with your request enclosing an SAE. An education officer can advise students wishing to apply to Italian universities.

Contact: The Italian Cultural Institute, 39 Belgrave Square, London SW1X 8NX

Tel: 020 7235 1461

Travel and adventure in the UK and abroad

Chapter 12
Planning and preparation

Most of the information in these chapters relates to foreign travel, as backpacking around the UK is a much simpler exercise, but we do include some useful sources of information for within these shores. Whatever your travel intentions, you need to think through your aims and objectives for the period.

- In terms of impressing potential future employers, it is often useful to gain some work experience during your year out - you could either include it in your travel experience, or leave time before or after your trip to spend time in a workplace situation. You may need a period of paid employment to subsidise your travels anyway.

- For your own sake, be as thorough as you can at the planning and preparation stage. This can save you many disappointments and a lot of wasted time while you are away.

- If you are travelling abroad, do your homework on the subject of work permits, visas, health requirements, cultural differences etc.

- Try to learn at least a few words of the language or languages of any foreign countries you are visiting. It is usually appreciated, even if it's not enough to be very useful!

ISIC/IYTC card

Travel abroad can be expensive, but all people over the age of 12 who are in full-time education are eligible for an International Student Identity Card (ISIC). The ISIC is the only document that is internationally accepted as proof of your student status, and it entitles holders to reductions on travel fares and on charges to places of interest in the UK and abroad. ISIC cards cost £6 (£6.50 if applying by post) and applicants also receive a free copy of the *ISIC World Travel Handbook*. There is also an ISIC helpline, a special emergency service, which can be used from anywhere in the world. Details are on the card.

An application for an ISIC card must be accompanied by:

- valid proof of full-time student status (e.g. a letter from your school/college/university on dated and headed paper or a clear copy of a National Union of Students (NUS) membership card)

- a passport photograph.

ISIC cards are obtainable from student travel offices, NUS branches or through mail-order.

The International Youth Travel Card (IYTC) is available for part-time students who are 25 years old or under. The application process is similar to the ISIC but you must provide proof of age (e.g. birth certificate or passport) rather than evidence of full-time student status.

Student travel agencies

A few agencies, such as usit CAMPUS specialise in offering travel services to students and under-26-year-olds. This agency deals with European and worldwide destinations, and can arrange coach, train or air travel plus travel insurance. Flexible tickets are available from usit CAMPUS, which means that dates and destinations can be changed. There are offices throughout the UK, many based on university campuses. The agency also has offices abroad which can offer help when overseas. For more details, call usit CAMPUS at their national call centre on telephone: 0870 240 1010 (or visit their website: www.usitcampus.co.uk).

STA Travel (telephone: 0870 1600 599, website: www.statravel.co.uk) offers discounted travel to students and those under 26. There are offices in most major UK cities.

Useful guides

Regional Tourist Boards can provide a lot of useful information about parts of the UK, including lists of bed and breakfast accommodation and campsites. The British Tourist Authority (telephone: 020 8846 9000) has the addresses of all the Regional Tourist Boards. Local tourist information centres are a mine of information as you travel. Membership of the Ramblers Association brings benefits to potential long-distance walkers, and books such as the Wainwright series of fell-walking guides have been used successfully by a couple of generations of walkers.

The Lonely Planet and *Rough Guide* series of guides to many countries and areas of the world provide excellent information on budget accommodation and places to eat as well as information on travel, sightseeing and potential problems and hazards. The series are available in most major bookshops and both have websites (www.lonelyplanet.com and www.roughguides.com).

There are a lot of other good guidebooks; you can spend many happy hours browsing in your local bookshop. There's also a lot of information to be gleaned from books about your chosen destinations by travel writers such as Dervla Murphy, Bill Bryson, Paul Theroux or Redmond O'Hanlon.

Insurance

When travelling abroad, make sure that you organise comprehensive travel insurance before you go which covers medical fees and loss of personal belongings. For Europe, remember to complete the certificate of entitlement to reciprocal healthcare in the European Union (E111), available from post offices, before you leave the UK. The International Student Insurance Service (ISIS) provides reasonably priced insurance cover for young people. Details of ISIS are available from Endsleigh Insurance Services Ltd (telephone: 01242 582563), or it has branches in many universities and most big towns. Columbus Insurance Services Ltd in London (telephone: 020 7225 1733) specialises in travel insurance, or you'll find other companies advertising in the travel sections of newspapers and magazines. Shop around for the best deal for you; look out for policies which cover travel for extended periods – often up to 24 months. Some workcamps and voluntary agencies arrange insurance cover for people taking part in their projects but this is not always the case. Most tour operators offer their own insurance policies.

Visas

You will need to organise visas to enter most countries outside Europe. In some cases, you will need to arrange the visa before you enter the country, either in the UK or in the country you visit previously. Sometimes, you will be issued with a visa on entry to the country and will be allowed to stay there for a few months. In many countries, visas issued will just allow you to travel. Work visas will normally be more difficult to arrange. Before you go, check visa requirements with the relevant embassies based in London (see list of embassy addresses in Part 5 – to save you time, if the embassy you need to contact has a website, you may be able to print off a visa application form). As an example of potential difficulties, some Arab countries won't issue you with a visa if your passport shows that you have been to Israel.

Inoculations

For many countries, particularly in Asia, South America and Africa, you will need to have inoculations such as tetanus, hepatitis and polio and you will need to take malaria tablets with you. It may take a month or more to complete a series of inoculations, so make sure you think about this early. Check inoculations required with your GP's surgery, or ring the MASTA (Medical Advisory Services for Travellers Abroad) travellers' healthline. MASTA is a database validated by the London School of Hygiene and Tropical Medicine. The number to call is 090 6822 4100 and lines are open 24 hours a day, (or ring 023 9250 5700 if your journey includes more than six countries). Calls cost 60p a minute and you will be sent a health brief specifically tailored to your journey. You will also be given information about immunisations, malaria advice, as well as any Foreign Office and latest health news.

The Department of Health publishes a useful booklet called *Health Advice for Travellers*, but you will still need to check that the information is up-to-date.

Finally, in some countries, you have to carry paperwork proving you have had certain vaccinations such as yellow fever.

Finance

Calculating how much money you need to take with you is a bit like asking how long is a piece of string. Try to calculate how much you're likely to spend by finding out approximate costs of travel and accommodation, and by researching the costs of living in the countries to which you intend to travel. Make sure that you have enough money to cover all eventualities (including illness and accidents) – or, at least, means of getting money sent to you in emergencies. Traveller's cheques are a fairly safe way to carry money. If you keep details of all your traveller's cheques they can be replaced if they are lost or stolen. Try to take a mixture of large and small denominations. Some cash in the local currency can be useful when you first arrive - although there is usually an opportunity to change a traveller's cheque at airports or ferry terminals, etc. A credit card such as Visa or Mastercard can be useful if you get into financial difficulties. You can use your 'hole-in-the-wall' cash card in many parts of the world.

Safety

Even in this country, mountainous areas or moorland can be dangerous without the proper equipment and preparation. Find out about the places you will be visiting before setting off, so that you know of any difficulties likely to present themselves. Contact the Foreign Office if you have any concerns about the political climate of an area. In some of the recommended foreign travel guide books you will find particular sections on dealing with hazards for women travellers.

Whether male or female, don't be too trusting so that you put yourself in awkward situations. Common sense is important, especially when you are travelling alone. Wear comfortable shoes so that you can run or walk quickly if necessary. Always let someone know where you are going and when you will be back. Ensure that you know local emergency numbers and, if possible, carry a mobile phone (but check it will work in the area). If travelling by bus, sit near the driver. Try to have your first night's accommodation booked before your arrival and aim to get there before dark. As far as possible, dress according to the cultural norm of the country you are visiting so you do not cause offence or attract unwelcome attention. Act confidently, you are less likely to appear vulnerable.

In tropical or developing countries, you need to be careful about food and water. Ice in drinks and food that is either uncooked, or cooked and then left standing, are worth avoiding.

Useful things to take with you

Below is a list of some of the things you might need to take, particularly if you are going to tropical countries:

- backpack or daysack
- money belt
- sheet sleeping bag
- inflatable pillow
- padlock
- malaria tablets
- medical kit including sterile needles
- sewing/repair kit
- ecologically-friendly travel detergent
- rehydration mixture (for severe diarrhoea)
- vitamin tablets
- traveller's cheques
- Visa/Mastercard or another internationally recognised credit card
- mosquito repellent (in some countries a mosquito net, electric anti-mosquito plug or smoke coils to use in your room at night could be useful)
- sunscreen and aftersun lotion
- guide books and maps
- toilet roll
- phrasebooks
- water purifying tablets
- salt tablets
- sunhat and good quality sunglasses
- walking boots or shoes
- small gifts to repay kindnesses

- and finally - as Michael Palin found out during his TV series - a universal bath plug.

It is likely that space and weight will be limited, so don't pack too much. If you know that clothes are going to be cheap where you are visiting, consider taking limited supplies. You can then buy and give away T-shirts etc as you go.

The following profile illustrates the need for careful planning and provides some useful tips:

Profile **Karen & Joe Harding**

Travelling the world

'After being married for less than one year, Joe (my husband) and I decided that we wanted a break. We felt that we had got into a bit of a rut, were not enjoying our jobs, and the mortgage we had for the house that we had bought four years ago was still a big financial burden. After all, weren't we a bit young to have so much responsibility? We felt we were at a crossroads in our careers, and lives – carry on as we had been or go away then come back to a fresh start. With this on our minds and our insatiable desire for endless sunshine, we decided to travel the world.

We chose to travel independently and booked flights and a couple of hotels. Our main destination was Australia and we got a 6-stop ticket around the world. Our first stops were Singapore and Bali, which we planned as more of a package holiday with hotels and trips booked before we left. Our next stop was Perth, Western Australia, then Sydney. Whilst in Australia, we travelled around by bus, train and on various 'backpacker' trips, to see all of the sights. We did some fruit picking, labouring and reception work to finance our travels. We then travelled to New Zealand where we ran out of money. Rescued by our parents, we decided to cut this stage short and go straight to Vancouver, Canada – our last destination. We hired a campervan to visit the Rockies.

We planned to do this trip over seven months, and only cut it short by two weeks, because of our finances. Money was the only real difficulty we encountered; we had expected to be able to earn more whilst in Oz. However poor, we felt that we gained a great deal from our time out. We had time to make plans and goals for our future; we learnt more about each other; we made lots of friends; saw places we would not have otherwise seen; had a fantastic time; and had the chance to make a fresh start when we returned. Now that we have returned, Joe has started as a trainee plumber, and I am about to start a postgraduate course in careers guidance, after temping during the summer.

Our top tips are – book accommodation in advance (even hostels). Take a credit card for bookings (whether you pay with your card or not). Buy multi-trip tickets – they are far cheaper and flexible. Set up your email account before you go – it is cheaper than phone calls. Use your British bank account to withdraw money as you go, rather than take too many travellers cheques. Finally, buy a good travel guide, e g. Lonely Planet – absolutely essential.'

Chapter 13
The journey

So, you've researched your destination country. You know all there is to know about its visa and health requirements, and you've found out about travel insurance policies. The big decision now is whether you want to travel independently or as part of an organised group.

Independent travel

You may decide to go it alone and to organise your travels independently. If this is what you decide, make sure that you plan ahead and that you have enough money to finance your travels. Making arrangements as you go in distant lands can be a headache, but it is also part of the experience of real travel! The Independent Travellers' World exhibition, which takes place early each year in London, includes talks and videos about other people's experiences.

How you choose to travel will obviously depend on your budget and the time you have available.

By train

Within the UK, you can purchase an All-Line Rover ticket offering unlimited travel for seven days for £315, or for 14 days for £480. If you have a Young Person's Railcard you get one-third off most rail fares. Ask at your nearest station or phone 0845 748 4950 for train information.

Rail Europe offers two main cheap rail passes. These are the Inter-Rail Pass and the EuroDomino Pass.

At the time of writing, if you are under 26, with the Inter-Rail Pass it is possible to travel around all the zones listed below for £229, just two zones for £169, or three zones for £199, each valid for a month; or for one zone, valid for 22 consecutive days, for £129. If you are 26 or over, you can still buy an Inter-Rail Pass but they cost more e.g. to travel around all the zones costs £319.

The zones are:

- Republic of Ireland
- Finland, Norway, Sweden
- Austria, Denmark, Germany, Switzerland
- Croatia, Hungary, Poland, the Slovak and Czech Republics
- Belgium, France, Luxembourg, the Netherlands

- Morocco, Portugal, Spain
- Greece, Italy, Slovenia, Turkey
- Bulgaria, Romania, Macedonia, Yugoslavia.

EuroDomino Passes can be purchased for from three to eight days' travel within a one-month period in any one of a number of European countries. For further information about these and other discounts, contact Rail Europe (telephone: 08705 848848, website: raileurope.co.uk).

If you are travelling by train outside Europe, it is worth finding out about the various types of train and classes of travel. Always opt for the best you can afford, especially if you have to cover long distances.

By bike

There is a lot of information available about cycle routes throughout the UK. This can be a cheap and healthy way of seeing the country. Sustrans offers information about routes within the UK (telephone: 0117 926 8893, website: www.sustrans.org.uk).

Membership of the Cyclists' Touring Club costs £10 if you are under 27, and £27 if you are aged 27 or over. Being a member entitles you to information about cycle routes worldwide (telephone: 01483 417217, website: www.ctc.org.uk).

Some tour operators and adventure holiday companies offer cycling holidays.

By plane

Look in the travel pages of weekend newspapers, on the internet or on Ceefax or Teletext for organisations offering competitively priced flights. Trailfinders deals with long- and short-haul around-the-world itineraries (telephone: 020 7938 3366, website: www.trailfinders.com). There are many other travel agents, usually based in London, that specialise in cheap long-haul flights. Some, such as STA Travel and usit CAMPUS (mentioned in more detail in chapter 12) particularly specialise in student travel. When booking a flight you need to shop around. Look out for the various tickets such as those that will give you several stops around the world, tickets that allow you at least one stop-over and those that enable you to fly into one destination and out of another. Once abroad, some airpasses include a certain number of domestic flights.

By coach

This can be the cheapest way of travelling, if you can cope with overnight trips and snatched moments of sleep. Watch out for various cheap offers from independent coach firms within the UK - especially on popular inter-city routes where competition is fierce. National Express Coaches have various discount cards e.g. for full-time students, young people under 25 and those aged 50 plus. The cards cost £9 for one year or £19 for three years and entitle you to up to a third off bus trips in the UK. For more details, contact National Express Coaches (telephone: 08705 808080, website: www.gobycoach.com).

There are a number of firms offering cheap coach travel around Europe. For instance, Eurolines sell passes which give you unlimited coach travel for up to 15, 30 or 60 days. The pass covers 46 cities in 26 countries. Prices are from £90 to £259 depending on the season, the number of days you will be travelling and your age. For more information, contact Eurolines (telephone: 08705 143219, or look on their website which is the same as for National Express above).

Greyhound buses in the USA and Canada offer passes for unlimited travel over periods from four to sixty days – they are good value if you intend to cover a lot of miles! You can buy a pass through a specialist agency e.g. Trailfinders, STA Travel or usit CAMPUS or visit their website: www.greyhound.com.

Hitching

Although 'hitching a ride' is a widely accepted method of travelling in most places, do take care. In some countries, drivers expect payment, so find out in advance how much this is likely to be. If possible, add a little extra as a tip.

Accommodation

Travel guides mentioned in the previous chapter list places to stay in different price ranges. If you are on a fairly tight budget, there are excellent inexpensive, clean and safe places to stay throughout the UK, Europe and beyond - especially for young people.

YHA (Youth Hostel Association)

If you are planning to travel around Britain and Europe, it would be worthwhile joining the YHA. YHA membership opens the door to 5000 youth hostels in 60 countries. Youth hostels are usually much cheaper than other accommodation available. If you buy an Inter-Rail Pass you may be able to join the YHA for a discounted price. The YHA produces handbooks of youth hostels throughout the world.

Contact: YHA, Trevelyan House, Dimple Road, Matlock, Derbyshire DE4 3YH.

Tel: 01629 592600. Fax: 01629 592702.
Email: customerservices@yha.org.uk
Website: www.yha.org.uk

YMCA (Young Men's Christian Association)

There are YMCA hostels all over the world which offer good value accommodation and welcome both women and men (it is not necessary to be a Christian to stay in them). You can order the *YMCA's World Directory* for £5 from the National Council of YMCAs (see below). This gives information on YMCAs worldwide.

Contact: The National Council of YMCAs, 640 Forest Road, London E17 3DZ.

Tel: 020 8520 5599. Fax: 020 8509 3190.

Email: info@england.ymca.org.uk

Website: www.ymca.org.uk

Camping

You'll have no trouble locating official campsites in most parts of the world. Unofficial camping can be a problem in some countries; you may find yourself being moved on by the authorities. Check the guidebooks mentioned in chapter 12 for information about campsite availability. Local tourist information centres will have lists of sites.

Bed and breakfast

This essentially British way of holiday-making can also be found in many other parts of the world. Local tourist information centres in the UK will have lists of private houses, pubs or small hotels which offer very reasonable accommodation, or National Tourist Offices of other countries may have information.

Homestays/exchanges

Organisations which arrange student exchanges are listed in chapter 11. A possibility for home-owners is house exchange organised independently or through an agency.

Organised adventurous and exploratory travel

There are a number of tour operators that specialise in organising small group exploratory holidays and adventurous travel to areas in Asia, Africa and South America. An example of a well-established tour operator in this field is Exodus Travels (telephone: 020 8675 5550, website: www.exodus.co.uk). They organise from two- to thirty-week trips on which participants are expected to be flexible and prepared to get involved. Some other well-known tour operators include Explore (telephone: 01252 344161), Guerba (telephone: 01373 826611), Travelbag Adventure (telephone: 01420 541007) and The Imaginative

Traveller (telephone: 020 8742 8612). Most of their bookings are made direct. There are some independent travel agencies, such as Trailfinders in London (mentioned earlier in this chapter), which specialise in these and other similar operators. You will usually find plenty of advertisements in the weekend newspapers. You often have the option of travelling on the group flight from the UK, or booking the land-only part of the trip, which means you can travel with the airline of your choice or incorporate the tour into your wider travels.

The Association of Independent Tour Operators (telephone: 020 8607 9080) publishes an annual directory of their members, which include adventure holiday operators and other non-mass tourism companies. Watch out for the Independent Travellers' World exhibition which, despite its name, is also a showcase for independent tour operators.

What it's like

This type of tour is ideal if you do not have a lot of time to spare but want to see as much of a country as possible. You may pay a bit more than you would if travelling independently, but then you don't have to queue for tickets, work out an itinerary, search for campsites or cheap hotels or find your own way back to the airport after running out of cash! The tour operators can offer advice about inoculations and visas, and you also have the security of travelling in a group, which can be particularly reassuring for lone females. The majority of people on these trips are travelling alone; couples are quite rare. Some operators have upper age limits, but many will take people of any age providing they are fit enough to cope with the demands of a particular trip. Some trips include trekking, whitewater rafting, horseriding, cycling or sailing. Accommodation may be simple hotels, tents, local village houses, rice barges or any combination of these. Some holiday companies organise trips where your holiday accommodation is with a family. There's something for everyone.

Groups - and leaders - vary enormously. There can be problems with clashes of personalities, people not pulling their weight on camping trips, and the 'free spirits' who wander off and get lost, keeping the rest of the group waiting and giving leaders some anxious moments! If you are one of the latter, perhaps you should stick to independent travel after all - although there are usually plenty of opportunities during a trip to explore on your own. A few weeks of group travel can be a welcome break from a solitary existence if you are travelling alone for several months.

On the whole, you are likely to find that people who choose the same trip will have a similar outlook and interests, so most groups gel pretty well and lasting friendships may be forged.

The following organisations may also be of interest.

The Sail Training Association (STA)

The STA runs adventure training courses all year round for people aged 16-24, on the *Stavros S Niarchos* and *Prince William*, the 60-metre brigs built to replace the famous tall ships, *Sir Winston Churchill* and *Malcolm Miller*. The voyages are fun, hard work and exciting.

During the spring, summer and autumn, the ships sail in Northern European waters; each two-week voyage sails up to 1000 miles and visits two or three foreign ports.

During the winter and spring, one tall ship sails to the warm water off the west coast of Africa, undertaking 10- or 11-day voyages in the Canary Islands and the Azores.

Each ship needs a full crew of 67 to sail. Everyone on board forms a vital part of the team to hoist sails, set them to catch the wind, tack or gybe the ship, stow the sails when they are finished with, take the helm, keep a look out and many other activities. No special skills or experience are required.

All voyages qualify for the residential section of the Duke of Edinburgh's Gold Award.

Voyages cost about £70 per day, fully inclusive. However the voyages can cost more than some young people can afford. The STA has a network of volunteer support groups, nationwide who may well be able to help by offering cash grants or help in finding a sponsor.

Contact: Sail Training Association, 2a The Hard, Portsmouth, Hampshire PO1 3PT.

Tel: 023 9283 2055. Fax: 023 9281 5769.

Email: tallships@sta.org.uk

Website: www.sta.org

WEXAS International

Worldwide travellers might be interested in joining Wexas International. This organisation makes awards totalling £2000 to approved group expeditions through the Royal Geographical Society Award Scheme.

Members of WEXAS benefit from special rates for immunisation, flights, insurance, hotels and car hire, as well as having access to Discoverers' holidays and receiving *Traveller* magazine. The World Discoverers' Programme combines a selection of round-the-world customised flights and tours with a variety of trips. Information on these holidays is available in the WEXAS *Travel Planner* brochure. WEXAS also publishes *The Traveller's Handbook* (available at discount to members) and two companion guides, *The Traveller's Healthbook* and *The Traveller's Internet Guide*.

The Traveller's Handbook (price £14.99 from bookshops) provides information on expeditions and adventure holidays plus advice for the independent traveller. It includes details on how to plan a trip, where to go, airline tickets, what equipment you will need, where to stay, what to do when things go wrong, e.g. theft, jungle survival. There are also useful contact addresses including consulates and organisations that arrange expeditions and adventure holidays.

Contact: WEXAS International, 45-49 Brompton Road, Knightsbridge, London SW3 1DE.

Tel: 020 7589 3315. Fax: 020 7589 8418.

Email: mship@wexas.com

Website: www.travelleronline.com

Expeditions

If you can raise the finances and sponsorship, you could spend a few months on an expedition in one of the developing regions of the world. This would involve group travel and you could work on a social or environmental project. Raleigh International, Trekforce, VentureCo Worldwide, Quest Overseas and others, where expeditions are combined with voluntary work, are listed in chapter 10. Organisations, such as the Wilderness Trust and Travellers Worldwide, which offer learning experiences, are described in chapter 11. Other organisations are:

Brathay Exploration Group Trust Ltd

The Trust arranges expeditions to countries as varied as Belize and Iceland, including ecological field studies, social development or community work. They also organise expeditions to remoter parts of Britain, and leadership courses. The Trust received a Royal Geographical Society medal in 1997 for services to exploration and youth adventurous activities.

Each expedition has a fully inclusive fee which is available in the Trust's detailed programme and can also be found on their website. Applicants should be aged between 16 and 23.

Contact: Brathay Exploration Group Trust Ltd, Brathay Hall, Ambleside, Cumbria LA22 0HP.

Tel/fax: 015394 33942.

Email: admin@brathayexploration.org.uk

Website: www.brathayexploration.org.uk

BSES Expeditions

Founded in 1932 by Surgeon Commander G. Murray Levick, a member of Scott's 1910 Antarctic expedition, the Society provides opportunities for young people to take part in challenging, exploratory projects in areas such as the Arctic, sub-Arctic, Antarctic, Kenya, Sinai, Papua New Guinea, India, Namibia, Zimbabwe, Queensland, Tasmania and Botswana.

Expeditions usually last six or twelve weeks. Apply in the summer of the previous year. Members have to find costs of at least £2200, which is seen as part of the challenge, but the Society can give advice on this. Applicants need to be between 16½ and 20 years of age at the time of the expedition.

Contact: BSES Expeditions, at the Royal Geographical Society, Kensington Gore, London SW7 2AR.

Tel: 020 7591 3141. Fax: 020 7591 3140.

Email: bses@rgs.org

Website: www.bses.org.uk

Dorset Expeditionary Society Ltd

The Dorset Expeditionary Society is a registered charity which promotes adventure challenge for young people. Up to six overseas expeditions to remote areas of the world are approved each year. Costs range from £600 - £2200 for three to five weeks. There is also a training programme for young members and social events in the UK.

The best time to apply is between September and November for the following year. You need to be under 21, although those older are considered. Previous expedition experience is not necessary provided you are fit and healthy. A sense of humour and determination are helpful!

Contact: Dorset Expeditionary Society Ltd, c/o Budmouth Technology College, Chickerell Road, Weymouth, Dorset DT4 9SY.

Tel/fax: 01305 775599

Email: dorsetexp@wdi.co.uk

Website: www.dorsetexp.co.uk

World Challenge Expeditions

World Challenge Expeditions run a variety of challenging and developmental programmes for students aged 16-24 to do in their gap year or school or university holidays.

Team Challenge is a four- or six-week expedition focusing on a trek in a challenging environment and worthwhile and rewarding project work. Destinations include East Africa, the Andes and Amazon and the Himalayas.

First Challenge offers a challenging overseas 8, 10, or 14-day expedition to destinations such as Morocco or Poland designed to unlock leadership potential.

Leadership Challenge involves an action packed, fun and stimulating UK-based expedition specifically to develop skills that are valued by universities and future employers.

Contact: World Challenge Expeditions, Black Arrow House, 2 Chandos Road, London NW10 6NF.

Tel: 020 8728 7272.

Email: welcome@world-challenge.co.uk

Website: www.world-challenge.co.uk

Compare and contrast...

Just to give a taste of different ways of travelling in India, two of the authors of this book recount their own experiences below.

Profile Tessa Doe

Southern India on an organised expedition

'Whilst never (yet) having taken the luxury of a year out, I have travelled with several firms that specialise in small-group study tours or adventure holidays, on trips of between two and four weeks - usually over the Christmas period - a good time to be as far away from the UK as possible.

One of my most memorable journeys was three weeks on an Exodus truck expedition through southern India, starting in Bombay, down the west coast to Kerala and then across and up to Madras. Truck travel is an experience in itself. You are open to the elements, the smells, the noise and the dust, and subject to the whims of the rear suspension. It's the only way to travel.

Because this tour only ran two or three times a year, and went to places off the usual tourist map, the arrival of twenty assorted, dishevelled westerners in an open-sided truck caused reactions varying from incomprehension to uncontrollable hilarity. Almost without exception, we were welcomed with a warmth and tolerance that we probably did not deserve. When the truck driver misjudged the width of the road and dislodged a few roof tiles, the owner's only reaction was: 'No problem!', and a cheery wave.

India gets under one's skin. The contrasts of beauty and squalor, of lushness and poverty, of vast landscapes and overcrowded cities, and the sense of history, ancient cultures and spirituality are overwhelming. Your senses are swamped by colour, noise and scents (pleasant and unpleasant). Busy markets, marauding monkeys, sacred cows among the traffic, sari-clad women carrying gleaming brass pots on their heads, and highly decorated temple elephants delicately accepting coins with their trunks, are among my most vivid memories - not to mention three curries a day!

We stayed in basic hotels. Some were excellent. In others, clean linen and spotless bathrooms were further down the list of priorities than in the UK. Several of the group did pick up bugs of varying degrees of seriousness.

We often left one town before dawn and arrived at the next destination after dark, breaking the long day's drive with a picnic breakfast and lunch on the way, which usually attracted quite an audience of locals, their dogs and their livestock. We all took it in turns to shop, cook and wash up.

Some of the group had been on the truck for the three weeks prior to our journey, as it travelled from Katmandhu to Bombay. Several were continuing to travel, either on another organised group expedition or independently.

To sum up, if you have months to spare and you really enjoy making your own arrangements and travelling alone, then an organised adventure or discovery holiday is not for you. If you prefer the security of travelling in a group, and are more than happy for someone else to have the hassle and responsibility, then this is an ideal way of seeing a bit of the world.'

Profile **Helen Evans**
Independently around India

'When so many of us visit overseas destinations under the auspices of arranged travel packages, the most surprising thing about travelling independently in a very different country like India is the sheer effort and mental energy it can take. Even buying a train or bus ticket can prove a time-consuming and challenging experience, when unfamiliar with local systems or the language! I remember on more than one occasion feeling ready to give up the struggle, after negotiating several long queues, and being provided with several totally conflicting, albeit well meant, bits of information! However, the sense of achievement of successfully navigating your own way around cannot be underestimated.

Using public transport, of course, brings you into slightly closer contact with the local people, and you can learn a lot. Be prepared to be objects of some curiosity, however. My female travelling companion and I were continually plied with questions, often of a very direct nature! Are you married? Have you got children? How big is your family? On a journey of 10-12 hours, it all, at times, got too much and, I am ashamed to say, I remember taking refuge in my personal stereo. That brings me to another aspect of independent travel - the uncomfortable sense of knowing that your camera, watch and backpack alone probably cost more than most of your fellow passengers earn in a year - or longer. You come face to face, literally, with the world's inequalities.

You have to cope with the unexpected. I recall one very long overnight bus journey in Southern India. A burst tyre was the first unscheduled stop, but everyone waited patiently while it was fixed! Later on, at 3.00 a.m., the bus was impounded at a police checkpoint, as it hadn't got the necessary paperwork. We were all left high and dry. I'll never know quite where we were, but it was miles from anywhere!

Arriving can be an experience in itself. The typical scenario saw us newly arrived at a train or bus station, Lonely Planet Guide in hand, being besieged by a clamour of people vying for our custom. 'I have a very good hotel!'; 'Taxi - taxi - come this way please!'; 'You want guide - I take you to all the sights!'. I recall having to flee at one point while two rickshaw drivers argued furiously about which had engaged us first, egged on by a crowd who all joined in!

Perhaps you feel this illustrates the disadvantages of independent travel - it depends how you look at it. I feel it offers a lot - freedom, the opportunity to discover new places through your own efforts, the chance to meet different people, and to learn about yourself. Not to forget the magic of drawing into a railway station with platforms full of colour and life, and delicious items of food being passed in through the windows...'

5

Appendices

Appendix 1
Embassy addresses

Useful information on working and studying in Europe and worldwide can be gathered by contacting embassies. When contacting embassies, you will need, in most cases, to ask to speak to the labour office for information on employment and the cultural or education department for information on study. Generally, embassies can provide information relating to employment in the country they represent, information about visa requirements etc, but most do not deal with job vacancies. They usually provide information on study and language courses.

The contact details of embassies of countries popular with people taking a year off are given below. Addresses of countries not listed can be found in *The London Diplomatic List* and *Whitakers Almanack*, available in reference libraries.

AUSTRALIA

Australian High Commission
Australia House
Strand
London WC2B 4LA
Tel: 020 7379 4334
www.australia.org.uk

AUSTRIA

Austrian Embassy
18 Belgrave Mews West
London SW1X 8HU
Tel: 020 7235 3731
www.austria.org.uk

BELGIUM

Belgian Embassy
103 Eaton Square
London SW1W 9AB
Tel: 020 7470 3700
www.belgium-embassy.co.uk

BOTSWANA

Botswana High Commission
6 Stratford Place
London W1C 1AY
Tel: 020 7499 0031

BRAZIL

Brazilian Embassy
32 Green Street
London W1K 7AT
Tel: 020 7499 0877
www.brazil.org.uk

CANADA

Canadian High Commission
Macdonald House
1 Grosvenor Square
London W1X 0AB
Tel: 020 7258 6600
www.canada.org.uk

CHINA

Embassy of the People's Republic of
China
49-51 Portland Place
London W1B 1JL
Tel: 020 7299 4049
www.chinese-embassy.org.uk

CZECH REPUBLIC

Embassy of the Czech Republic
26-30 Kensington Palace Gardens
London W8 4QY
Tel: 020 7243 1115
www.czech.org.uk

DENMARK

Royal Danish Embassy
55 Sloane Street
London SW1X 9SR
Tel: 020 7333 0200
www.denmark.org.uk

ECUADOR

Embassy of Ecuador
Flat 3B
3 Hans Crescent
London SW1X 0LS
Tel: 020 7584 1367

FINLAND

Embassy of Finland
38 Chesham Place
London SW1X 8HW
Tel: 020 7838 6200
www.finemb.org.uk

FRANCE

French Embassy
58 Knightsbridge
London SW1 7JT
Tel: 020 7073 1000
www.ambafrance.org.uk

GERMANY

Embassy of the Federal Republic of
Germany
23 Belgrave Square
London SW1X 8PZ
Tel: 020 7824 1300
www.german-embassy.org.uk

GREECE

Embassy of Greece
1A Holland Park
London W11 3TP
Tel: 020 7229 3850
www.greekembassy.org.uk

HUNGARY

Embassy of the Republic of
Hungary
35 Eaton Place
London SW1X 8BY
Tel: 020 7235 5218
www.huemblon.org.uk

ICELAND

Embassy of Iceland
2A Hans Street
London SW1X 0JE
Tel: 020 7259 3999
www.iceland.org.uk

INDIA

High Commission of India
India House
Aldwych
London WC2B 4NA
Tel: 020 7836 8484
www.hcilondon.org

INDONESIA

Embassy of the Republic of
Indonesia
38 Grosvenor Square
London W1K 2HW
Tel: 020 7499 7661
www.indonesianembassy.org.uk

IRELAND

Embassy of Ireland
17 Grosvenor Place
London SW1X 7HR
Tel: 020 7235 2171

ISRAEL

Embassy of Israel
2 Palace Green
Kensington
London W8 4QB
Tel: 020 7957 9500
www.israel-embassy.org.uk

ITALY

Italian Embassy
14 Three Kings Yard
Davies Street
London W1Y 2EH
Tel: 020 7312 2200
www.embitaly.org.uk

JAPAN

Embassy of Japan
101-104 Piccadilly
London W1J 7JT
Tel: 020 7465 6500
www.embjapan.org.uk

KENYA

Kenya High Commission
45 Portland Place
London W1N 4AS
Tel: 020 7636 2371
www.kenyahighcommission.com

LITHUANIA

Embassy of the Republic of
Lithuania
84 Gloucester Place
London W1U 6AU
Tel: 020 7486 6401

LUXEMBOURG

Embassy of Luxembourg
27 Wilton Crescent
London SW1X 8SD
Tel: 020 7235 6961

MALAWI

High Commission for the Republic
of Malawi
33 Grosvenor Street
London W1K 4QT
Tel: 020 7491 4172

MALAYSIA

Malaysian High Commission
45 Belgrave Square
London SW1X 8QT
Tel: 020 7235 8033

NEPAL

Royal Nepalese Embassy
12A Kensington Palace Gardens
London W8 4QU
Tel: 020 7229 1594
www.nepembassy.org.uk

NEW ZEALAND

New Zealand High Commission
New Zealand House
80 Haymarket
London SW1Y 4TQ
Tel: 020 7930 8422
www.nzembassy.com

NORWAY

Royal Norwegian Embassy
25 Belgrave Square
London SW1X 8QD
Tel: 020 7591 5500
www.norway.org.uk

PAKISTAN

High Commission for the Islamic
Republic of Pakistan
35-36 Lowndes Square
London SW1X 9JN
Tel: 020 7664 9200
www.pakmission-uk.gov.pk

PERU

Embassy of Peru
52 Sloane Street
London SW1X 9SP
Tel: 020 7235 1917
www.peruembassy-uk.com

POLAND

Embassy of the Republic of Poland
47 Portland Place
London W1N 4JH
Tel: 020 7580 4324
www.poland-embassy.org.uk

PORTUGAL

Portuguese Embassy
11 Belgrave Square
London SW1X 8PP
Tel: 020 7235 5331

RUSSIA

Embassy of the Russian Federation
13 Kensington Palace Gardens
London W8 4QX
Tel: 020 7229 3628

SLOVAKIA

Embassy of the Slovak Republic
25 Kensington Palace Gardens
London W8 4QY
Tel: 020 7313 6470
www.slovakembassy.co.uk

SOUTH AFRICA

High Commission for the Republic
of South Africa
South Africa House
Trafalgar Square
London WC2N 5DP
Tel: 020 7451 7299
www.southafricahouse.com

SPAIN

Spanish Embassy
39 Chesham Place
London SW1X 8SB
Tel: 020 7235 5555

SWEDEN

Embassy of Sweden
11 Montagu Place
London W1H 2AL
Tel: 020 7917 6400
www.swedish-embassy.org.uk

SWITZERLAND

Embassy of Switzerland
16-18 Montagu Place
London W1H 2BQ
Tel: 020 7616 6000
www.swissembassy.org.uk

TANZANIA

High Commission for the United
Republic of Tanzania
43 Hertford Street
London W1J 7DB
Tel: 020 7499 8951
www.tanzania-online.gov.uk

THAILAND

Royal Thai Embassy
29-30 Queen's Gate
London SW7 5JB
Tel: 020 7589 2944

THE NETHERLANDS

Royal Netherlands Embassy
38 Hyde Park Gate
London SW7 5DP
Tel: 020 7590 3200
www.netherlands-embassy.org.uk

TURKEY

Embassy of the Republic of Turkey
43 Belgrave Square
London SW1X 8PA
Tel: 020 7393 0202
www.turkishembassy-london.com

UNITED STATES OF AMERICA

American Embassy
24 Grosvenor Square
London W1A 1AE
Tel: 020 7499 9000
www.usembassy.org.uk

VIETNAM

Embassy of the Socialist Republic
of Vietnam
12 Victoria Road
London W8 5RD
Tel: 020 7937 1912

ZAMBIA

High Commission for the Republic
of Zambia
2 Palace Gate
Kensington
London W8 5NG
Tel: 020 7589 6655
www.zhcl.org.uk

ZIMBABWE

High Commission for the Republic
of Zimbabwe
Zimbabwe House
429 Strand
London WC2R 0QE
Tel: 020 7836 7755
www.zimbabwelink.com

Appendix 2
Bibliography

(Addresses of the main publishers are given at the end of this section.)
Many of these titles can be obtained from bookshops.
This list has been grouped by theme for ease of reference.

Options

An information pack about volunteering, working, travelling and teaching is produced by i–to–i. For a free copy, write to i–to–i, One Cottage Road, Headingley, Leeds LS6 4DD, or tel: 0870 333 2332.

PAYAway – Magazine about working holidays and travel. £8 for four issues. From 33 Upper Tooting Road, London SW17 7TR.

Travelling, Studying training and doing research, Working and Living within the European Union – free booklets available from Citizens First Information Line (tel: 0800 581591). There are also free factsheets on more specific issues.

A Year Between – published by Central Bureau, £9.99. Gives details of placements in industry, research, business, teaching, community service, youth work.

Eurofacts: Taking Time Out Abroad – a series of leaflets covering ways of taking some time out in other countries in Europe, produced by Careers Europe. Should be available for reference in careers centres and libraries.

Taking a Career Break – published by Vacation Work, £11.95. Opportunities for travel, work and adventure for people considering taking an extended break.

www.gapyear.com is a source of gap-year information in the UK, covering independent travel, work experience, volunteering, study programmes and 'doing your own thing'.

The Year Out Group is an association of gap-year providers offering information on opportunities in the UK and overseas. Details can be found on www.yearoutgroup.org

Scholarships and sponsorship

Charities Digest – Waterlow Legal Publishers, Paulton House, 8 Shepherdess Walk, London N1 7LB (tel: 020 7490 0049). Provides details and addresses of national and regional charities in the UK including organisations related to health and social welfare, housing, education and the environment as well as grant–making trusts and sources of help for people in need. £22.95, plus £2 p&p.

The Educational Grants Directory – available from Trotman, £18.95.

Educational Grants Advisory Service – 501–505 Kingsland Road, London E8 4AU. You can telephone for advice on 020 7249 6636 (Mondays, Wednesdays and Fridays, 10 am – 12 noon, and 2pm – 4pm), or send an SAE for details of charities and organisations that offer grants.

Engineering Opportunities – available free from the Institution of Mechanical Engineers, c/o Marketing and Communication Department, 1 Birdcage Walk, London SW1H 9JJ (tel: 020 7222 7899).

Everything You Wanted to Know About Sponsorship – published by Amoeba Publications, Lakeside Manor Farm, Crowland Road, Eye Green, Cambridgeshire PE6 7TT (tel: 01733 223113). £14.95.

The Grants Register – published by Macmillan Press Ltd, Brunel Road, Houndmills, Basingstoke, Hampshire RG21 6XS (tel: 01256 329242). £125. This is primarily targeted at undergraduates/graduates who require further professional or advanced vocational training.

Guide to Postgraduate Studentships in the Humanities – from the British Academy, 10 Carlton House Terrace, London, SW1Y 5AH (telephone: 020 7969 5200), and available on the website – www.ahrb.ac.uk

Sponsorship and Donations Yearbook – published by Hollis Directories Ltd, Harlequin House, 7 High Street, Teddington, Middlesex TW11 8EL (tel: 020 8977 7711). £110.

Springboard Sponsorship and Funding Directory – published by CRAC/Hobsons. £8.99.

Students' Money Matters – published by Trotman. £10.99. Information on finance for students including loans, a year out, sponsorships and bursaries.

Paid employment

The following are published by Vacation Work:

Working in Tourism: the UK, Europe and Beyond – £11.95.

Work Your Way Around the World – £12.95.

The Au Pair and Nanny's Guide to Working Abroad – £11.95.

Directory of Summer Jobs Abroad – £9.99 paperback, £15.95 hardback.

Directory of Summer Jobs in Britain – £9.99 paperback, £15.95 hardback.

World Volunteers – £10.99.

Live and Work in... Australia & New Zealand; Belgium; the Netherlands & Luxembourg; France; Germany; Italy; Russia & Eastern Europe; Saudi & the Gulf; Scandinavia; Spain & Portugal; USA & Canada – £10.99 each.

Internships 2002 – £18.95.

Summer Jobs USA 2002 – £12.95.

Teaching English Abroad – £12.95.

Working in Ski Resorts: Europe & North America – £10.99.

Working on Cruise Ships – £10.99.

The following are published by How To Books:

Teaching English as a Foreign Language – £9.99.

Getting a Job Abroad – £12.99.

Getting a Job in Europe – £9.99.

Teaching Abroad – £9.99.

Living and Working in... – a series of 14 titles, £9.99 to £12.99.

Overseas Jobs Express – fortnightly newspaper full of vacancies and articles about working abroad. Available on subscription from Overseas Jobs Express, Premier House, Shoreham Airport, Sussex BN43 5FF.

The following titles are available from Overseas Jobs Express, at the address above:

Teaching English Abroad – £12.99.

Working on Cruise Ships – £10.99.

Live and Work Abroad – £12.95.

Living and Working in America – £13.99.

Living and Working in Australia – £13.99.

Opportunities Abroad – bulletin of vacancies in development work, available from World Service Enquiry, Bon Marche Centre, Suite 233, 241 – 251 Ferndale Road, London SW9 8BJ.

Working Abroad (The Daily Telegraph Guide) – available from Trotman. £12.99.

Working Holidays Abroad – published by Trotman. £9.99.

Working Holidays – published by Central Bureau. £9.99.

Working in... (all EU countries) – free from the Overseas Placing Unit, Level 1, Rockington House, 123 West Street, Sheffield S1 4ER Tel: 0114 259 6052.

Voluntary work

Archaeology Abroad Bulletin – published twice a year by Archaeology Abroad (see entry in chapter 10), price £12.50 per annum. Lists overseas projects requiring volunteers.

Careers Europe – factsheets for those taking up voluntary work in Europe. Should be available for consultation in careers service libraries.

Spirit of Volunteering – information sheet from the National Centre for Volunteering (see chapter 7).

Voluntary Agencies Directory – available from the National Council for Voluntary Organisations, Regent's Wharf, 8 All Saints Street, London N1 9RL (tel: 020 7713 6161), £25 plus £5 p&p. Your local reference library should hold a copy.

Voluntary Work and Young People/Volunteer Action – information sheets available from the National Youth Agency (see chapter 7).

The International Directory of Voluntary Work – published by Vacation Work. £10.99 paperback, £15.95 hardback.

Kibbutz Volunteer – published by Vacation Work. £10.99.

Green Volunteers – published by Vacation Work. £10.99. For UK and worldwide opportunities.

Working in the Voluntary Sector – published by How To Books. £8.99.

Worldwide Volunteering for Young People – published by How To Books. £15.95.

Study

See the UK higher education handbooks such as CRAC's *Degree Course Guides*, *The UCAS Big Guide*, and the ECCTIS UK Course Discover database, for details of courses which include time spent overseas.

Experience Erasmus: the UK guide to Socrates–Erasmus Programmes 2002 – ISCO, 12a Princess Way, Camberley, Surrey GU15 3SP (tel: 01276 21188), £13 plus £2 p&p.

Study Abroad – published by UNESCO and available from The Stationery Office, Publications Centre, PO Box 276, London SW8 5DT (tel: 020 7873 0011), £17.50.

Study Europe 2002 – an International Guide, published by Hobsons. £9.99.

Time to Learn – published by City & Guilds London Institute, 1 Giltspur Street, London EC1A 9DD (tel: 020 7294 2850). Includes short courses and study holidays – mostly in the UK but also some abroad. £4.99 plus £1 p&p.

Travel

Lonely Planet – series of over 300 guide books available in most bookshops. They also publish a free quarterly newsletter called *Planet Talk*. Lonely Planet, The Barley Mow Centre, 10 Barley Mow Passage, Chiswick, London W4 4PH. (tel: 020 8742 3161.)

Rough Guides – another series of guide books particularly useful for independent travellers, available in most bookshops.

The Traveller's Handbook – published by WEXAS International, 45–49 Brompton Road, Knightsbridge, London SW3 1DE (tel: 020 7589 3315), £14.99. www.travelleronline.com

The *Traveller's Healthbook* at £7.50 and *The Traveller's Internet Guide* at £5 are also published by WEXAS International.

Spending the Year Abroad – published by How To Books. £9.99.

Travellers Survival Kit – a series of 15 guides, published by Vacation Work, £9.95 – £15.95.

Trailblazer: route guides for the adventurous traveller – including walking guides, rail guides and overland guides. Approximately £10–15 each. More details by telephoning 01428 605797 or on www.trailblazer-guides.com

The Virgin Student Travellers' Handbook: The Definitive Guide To Planning a Gap Year – published by Virgin, £12.99.

Wanderlust – magazine for travellers available on subscription or from newsagents.

Addresses of publishers most frequently referred to:

Central Bureau – 10 Spring Gardens, London SW1A 2BN. Tel: 020 7389 4004.

How to Books – Customer Services Department, Plymbridge Distributors Ltd, Estover Road, Plymouth, Devon PL6 7PY. Tel: 01752 202301. www.howtobooks.co.uk

For further information about the books, contact How To Books, 3 Newtec Place, Magdalen Road, Oxford OX4 1RE, or visit the website above.

Vacation Work – 9 Park End Street, Oxford OX1 1HJ. Tel: 01865 241978. www.vacationwork.co.uk

Trotman Publishing Ltd – Plymbridge Distributors Ltd, Estover Road, Plymouth PL6 7PY. Tel: 0870 900 2665. www.careers–portal.co.uk

For general enquiries, Tel: 020 8486 1160.

Hobsons plc – Customer Services, Plymbridge Distributors Ltd, Estover Road, Plymouth PL6 7PZ. Tel: 01752 202301. www.hobsons.com

(For further information about the books, contact Copy Sales Department, Hobsons plc, Challenger House, 42 Adler Street, London E1 1EE. Tel: 020 7958 5000, or visit the website above.)

Index

Country entries: Please note that countries are only listed in this index if specifically mentioned in the text. This does not mean that other organisations/topics do not operate in or relate to that country. Many organisations' entries describe their activities as 'worldwide' or 'overseas' and therefore are not indexed under separate countries.

Index of advertisers

The Student Helpbook series

Jobs and Careers after A Levels and equivalent advanced level qualifications

Opportunities for students leaving school or college at 18
£9.99   ISBN: 1 902876 15 6

NEW EDITION
CVs and Applications

For anyone who is applying for a job or college place
£10.99   ISBN: 1 902876 31 8

NEW EDITION
Student Life: A Survival Guide

For anyone beginning, or soon to begin, university or college
£10.99   ISBN: 1 902876 36 9

NEW EDITION
Excel at Interviews

New edition of this highly successful title, invaluable reading for students and jobhunters
£10.99   ISBN: 1 90287630 X

Careers with a Science Degree

Compulsory reading for anyone considering science at degree level
£9.99   ISBN: 1 873408 93 5

Careers with an Arts Degree

Compulsory reading for anyone considering arts at degree level
£9.99   ISBN: 1 873408 92 7

For further details please contact:

Customer Services, Lifetime Careers Publishing, 7 Ascot Court, White Horse Business Park, Trowbridge, BA14 0XA
Tel: 01225 716023; Fax: 01225 716025
Email: sales@wiltshire.lifetime-careers.co.uk